Marginal Medicine

Marginal Medicine

EDITED BY ROY WALLIS AND PETER MORLEY

THE FREE PRESS
A Division of Macmillan Publishing Co., Inc.
NEW YORK

The Free Press
A Division of Macmillan Publishing Co., Inc.
866 Third Avenue, New York, N.Y. 10022

Library of Congress Catalog Card Number: 76–43129

Printed in the United States of America

printing number

1   2   3   4   5   6   7   8   9   10

Library of Congress Cataloging in Publication Data
Main entry under title:

Marginal medicine.

    Bibliography: p.
    1. Therapeutic systems. 2. Therapeutic systems--
Social aspects. I. Wallis, Roy. II. Morley, Peter.
R733.M37 1976   615'.5   76-43129
ISBN 0-02-933740-2

Contents

Acknowledgments

The essays included in this volume are presented here for the first time. Chapter 5, however, represents an abridged version of Chapters 2 and 3 of Roy Wallis, *The Road to Total Freedom,* Heinemann Educational Books, London. While substantial new material has been added, the author and editors gratefully acknowledge the permission of Heinemann Educational Books to include a number of passages from this work.

The editors also wish to thank Richard Bland for his helpful comments on the manuscript, and Marion Speirs and Dorothy Buchan for their patience and skill in typing parts of the work.

R.W. and P.M.

Roy Wallis and Peter Morley

1

Introduction

While systematic techniques for the alleviation and cure of human ailments are as ancient as man himself, marginal medicine in western societies is, in a crucial sense, a recent phenomenon. Practices denigrated by medical men as 'quackery' have existed for centuries, of course, but *marginal* medicine can only be said to exist where there is a dominant medical orthodoxy widely regarded as effective and legitimate by the members of a society. That is, we can talk of orthodox medicine (and hence also of marginal medicine) only under the following conditions:

1 There exists an occupational group whose job it is to apply therapeutic procedures to the sick;

2 This group displays a high level of consensus concerning the causes of, and appropriate treatments for, most human ailments;

3 Its members are attributed a high degree of legitimacy by the client group, which regards them as peculiarly competent to treat the sick.

While the first condition has been met throughout history, the second and third conditions have been characteristic only of some small scale, traditional societies on the one hand, and medicine in advanced industrial societies over the last century or century and a half on the other hand.

In some small scale, traditional societies, the application of

9

medical knowledge and procedures of a specialized kind is the prerogative of an occupationally differentiated group considered to
possess uniquely efficacious means of managing illness. Disconcert-
ingly, it is western scientific medicine which typically occupies a
marginal position in this situation, and is viewed with suspicion by
the sick, and as illegitimate by the orthodox practitioner.

Most societies are, and have historically been, medically *plural-
istic*. Practitioners of various curing arts employing distinct concepts and techniques have competed for a clientele which accords
to none of them a status as uniquely competent or efficacious over
the general domain of human illness. Conditions of culture contact
and social change enhance the tendency towards pluralism in the
domain of medicine as in other spheres of social life. A growing
division of labour produces differences in life and work experience,
which lead to the emergence of competing views of man and
society and hence to differentiation in the way human problems
are conceived and managed.[1]

In western societies the attempt to create a consensus concerning
illness, its treatment, or the peculiar appropriateness of particular
occupational specialists to have a monopoly of that treatment, has
a lengthy history. A Royal College of Physicians has existed in
England since the sixteenth century, devoted in considerable
measure to the pursuit of that aim.[2] Not until the nineteenth
century, however, did it begin to achieve more than occasional
successes in this endeavour. Throughout the intervening period,
conflict both with other incorporated practitioners of the therapeutic arts – in particular the barbers and the apothecaries – and
with unincorporated practitioners was intense. Physicians for the
most part confined their healing activities to the ills of the relatively
wealthy; the inevitable result was the emergence of less prestigious
practitioners who dispensed their services and nostrums to the
more humble. But even among the rich and influential, the practitioner licensed by the Royal College was not viewed as necessarily
possessing greater knowledge or competence than the unlicensed
practitioner. The court and nobility were as likely to patronize unorthodox medical men, even maintaining a residual allegiance to
homeopathy long after the triumph of allopathic medicine.

The Industrial Revolution rapidly transformed both the demand for effective medical treatment and the ability of the profession to provide it. A major concomitant of the Industrial Revolution was greater mobility, both geographical, with the drift toward the urban areas, and social, as individuals moved between one status group and another. Geographical mobility and urbanization broke down the links of individuals with a stable traditional community and therefore with traditional ideas concerning their appropriate lot in life. Industrialization led to social mobility through the enormous expansion of the middle class and the gradual replacement of ascriptive criteria of birth and land ownership by achieved criteria of competence and ability as the bases of placement in the hierarchy of social stratification. Traditional resignation to one's life-circumstances was gradually replaced by a more democratic ethos in which the view became more prevalent that certain fundamental attributes of citizenship – the right to equality before the law, the right to participate in the exercise of political power, the right to certain minimal standards of health, income and happiness – were the prerogative of all adult members of the society.[3] The possibility of social progress and personal improvement led to the articulation of a range of demands, for universal suffrage on one hand, and for more effective and widely available medical resources on the other.

The practice of medicine is surrounded by a number of tensions and sources of potential social disruption. Terence Johnson has pointed out that

> Certain occupations are associated with particularly acute problems of uncertainty, where client or consumer judgement is particularly ineffective and the seeking of skilled help necessarily invites intrusion of others into intimate and vulnerable areas of the consumer's self- or group-identity. Medical practice, for example, intrudes into areas of culturally defined ritual significance such as birth and death.[4]

The provision of medical services is both threatening and a source of uncertainty. In a world of increasing occupational specialization and differentiation, the client becomes increasingly helpless in areas where he lacks expertise, and thus becomes more vulnerable to exploitation. Where the clientele of the expert is a small group of wealthy patrons, a high level of control remains possible, but with the emergence of a heterogeneous mass clientele for the services of the physician, personal and economic controls become less effective.[5] There thus arises a greater need for formal mechanisms of control, and a demand for state regulation.

Social control of the practice of medicine took two broad forms. First, the passage of state legislation established restrictions on who might or might not claim to be a medical practitioner acceptable to the state, and also limited the rights and privileges of those not acceptable. While the 1858 Medical Act in Britain restrained the erasure of an individual's name from the register of medical practitioners which it established 'on the grounds of his having adopted any theory of medicine or surgery', it nevertheless created a high degree of unity within the profession.[6] This and subsequent Acts increasingly arrogated to the registered practitioner a monopoly of certain practices and procedures which unregistered practitioners were not permitted to infringe. Second, control took the form of delegating to practitioners themselves the right to admit individuals or to exclude them from the recognized medical profession. While physicians had nominally possessed this right for centuries, its effective existence only dated from the change in public attitudes towards medicine, which occurred as it began, in the course of the nineteenth century, to achieve some clearly visible successes. Until well into the nineteenth century, the physician

> had little guarantee that his claim to professional knowledge would be borne out by any improvement in the patient's condition. Instead there seems to have been a tendency to rely on convincing the client of the efficacy of various universal nostra or panaceas. The public seem to have remained largely unconvinced of claims to professional expertise. . . .[7]

Industrialization, however, had also been associated with the accelerated growth of experimental science and technology which provided a means of testing systematically hypotheses concerning the causes and treatment of disease, hitherto dependent upon the doubtful insight of 'clinical experience'. It also provided an increasingly elaborate technical apparatus by means of which to apply the insights of experimental science. The bacteriological revolution of the nineteenth century clearly emerged in part from the technological concerns of industrial development, just as the pharmacopœia to cope with disease was closely associated with the development of chemistry as a scientifically central component of the industrial revolution.

The success of scientific medicine provided the foundation for a high level of consensus among physicians, particularly after the victory of the 'germ theory' of disease. The appearance of more routinely effective remedies for illness generated public support for physicians and sufficiently heightened their prestige as to legitimate the delegation of extensive professional controls over the occupational group and its practices to the practitioners themselves.

In America in particular, the legitimacy of practitioners had been limited by a laissez-faire attitude hostile to restriction on competition in medicine as elsewhere, an anti-intellectualism which did not credit doctors with any extensive esoteric knowledge and skills, and a tolerance for medical sects analogous to the constitutionally expressed tolerance for religious sects. These factors inhibited the recognition by the public of any unique claim to medical competence and authority by physicians, and it was not until, as Rodney Coe has observed a trifle rhetorically, 'the germ theory and its subsequent effective application to infectious diseases that medicine . . . regained control of its own destiny'.[8]

These political and scientific developments led to the dominance of scientifically-based medicine in advanced industrial societies.[9] The emergence of a broadly legitimated consensual orthodoxy among an organized medical profession, in turn, therefore, led to the emergence of marginal medicine. Marginal medicine in this sense refers to individuals and groups of occupational specialists concerned with the treatment of illness, but existing beyond the confines of the organized medical profession and its accepted ancillary professions. Almost inevitably marginal practitioners conduct their practice not merely outside the profession, its facilities and privileges, but also on the basis of divergent beliefs concerning the causes and appropriate practices for coping with illness. Where orthodox medical care is either not readily available or too expensive for large sections of the population, there arises the possibility of marginal medical practice, outside the recognized profession, but operating on principles derived from scientific medicine. The dispensing pharmacist, for example, may, if orthodox medical care is a scarce resource, diagnose and prescribe, albeit without the approval of the medical profession and, in some settings, illegally.

More generally, marginal medicine is based on theories of illness and treatment practices which are deviant from those of the orthodox medical practitioner. Since orthodox medicine is scientifically based and derives much of its rationale from the germ theory of disease, marginal medicine tends to provide alternative legitimations for its practices. It may derive these from what are seen as superior, more transcendental sources such as direct revelation from God, or through supernatural agencies of cure: the Divine Mind (Christian Science, New Thought), or the action of spiritual beings or powers (spiritualist healing, magical healing practices, exorcism, etc.). Marginal medicine may base its healing claims on theories and techniques which are held by practitioners not to be amenable to normal scientific testing (homeopathy, psychoanalysis), or to be equally 'scientific' but ignored by scientists dogmatically committed to an outmoded or partial set of concepts or theories (chiropractic, Dianetics).* The causal factors invoked in explanation of illness similarly tend to deviate from bacteriological orthodoxy. They may on the one hand be more mechanistic than those of orthodox medicine (osteopathy or chiropractic), depending upon the deleterious displacements of physical structure; or

---

* Chiropractic is a school of medicine founded by D. D. Palmer, an unlicensed physician in Iowa, but largely promoted by his son, B. J. Palmer, from 1895 onwards. D. D. Palmer believed that illnesses resulted solely from interference with the nervous system caused by slight dislocations, or 'subluxations', of the spinal column. Treatment rested on manipulation of the spinal column as a whole, thereby relieving pressure on nervous tissue.

more idealistic, depending upon psychological trauma or what are construed by adherents as simply mistaken beliefs (Dianetics, Christian Science), or the vitality of the life force (homeopathy).

However, there is a further sense in which the emergence of an orthodox consensus within medicine may be said to lead to the emergence of marginal medicine. The notion of a consensus entails that certain things are agreed to be right, proper or relevant to orthodox practitioners. Hence it also entails that certain other things are discounted, considered improper or construed as irrelevant. The very success of modern surgery and bacteriologically-informed medical practice informed by an elaborate technology of immunization and pharmacology has militated against the investment of training and resources in such forms of treatment as physical manipulation and psychotherapy which are quite likely to provide effective alleviation and even cure in the case of certain forms of illness. The lack of adequate orthodox medical care in such areas promotes the emergence of alternative, marginal therapies and practitioners committed to the treatment of disorder by such means.[10] An overconcentration on particular forms of treatment has led to a growing scepticism concerning some aspects of orthodox medicine, enhanced by the clear evidence of iatrogenic illness resulting from a misplaced faith in the efficacy of drugs and surgery. The sceptical client of the homeopath or the naturopath may comfort himself, in the face of the revelations concerning Thalidomide, with the thought that while his treatment may do him little good, it is unlikely to do him and others so much harm. As allopathic orthodox medicine has sought to secure its position, it has tended bitterly to attack the practitioner of marginal medical techniques and the system which he employs. The deviant is denigrated as a quack or charlatan, impugning at the same time both his practice and his motivations for pursuing it. In response to such

---

Later practitioners of chiropractic introduced a variety of other forms of treatment, including dietary and electrical therapy, although some practitioners remain faithful to pure chiropractic as advocated by Palmer. Practitioners exist in considerable quantity in virtually all major urban centres in North America, although their presence outside the United States and Canada is negligible.

Dianetics is discussed in detail in Chapter 5.

opposition, marginal medicine has tended to adopt a sectarian
character, both denying any legitimacy to orthodox medicine and,
at the same time, seeking to insulate its practitioners and clients
from contamination.

Just as new religious movements emerging in a society dominated by a single church tend to take on a sectarian character,
hostile to the church and its officials, and seeking to envelop their
own members in a safe, insulated community of believers, so new
medical movements may come to provide not merely medical care
for their clients, but instead develop a total world-view and culture
which guides and also defends the following in their contacts with
alien, dominant beliefs and institutions. Therapeutic systems
sometimes develop from religious beliefs (pentecostal, spiritualist,
and Christian Science healing) which provide a wider set of legitimations and cognitive defences, but in other cases they may
develop into religious or metaphysical systems which fulfil the
same functions (the development of Dianetics into Scientology is
one such case).

Marginal medicine is clearly not born into a static world.
Changes in its social environment, in the attitude of orthodox
practitioners and in their techniques, and in the attitudes and
techniques of its own practitioners and clients, may all lead to
alterations in marginal medicine. The more successful orthodox
allopathic medicine has proved to be in the alleviation of physical
suffering, the greater the pressure for effective means of coping
with psychological ills. In this area, scientific medicine has
achieved very limited success, and consequently, as John Lee and
Roy Wallis point out in papers included in this volume, the greater
the likelihood that new forms of marginal medicine will present
themselves as concerned primarily with psychosomatic and
psychological disability, or problems of interpersonal relationships.
The need inevitably persists, however, for some assurance of cure
in the case of those residual, often chronically degenerative,
physical disorders such as cancer for which orthodox medicine has
also yet to provide an adequate remedy.

The prestige and hegemony of science and scientific medicine
has reached such a level in recent years that the medical profession

has been able to afford to be less defensive concerning some of its unorthodox competitors. Those marginal practices which undertake substantial reforms in training and practice to incorporate the theories and techniques of scientific medicine are viewed with less hostility and rejection.[11] Osteopathy in America has virtually been absorbed into medical orthodoxy, and as Walter Wardwell indicates in Chapter 4, a limited rapprochement with chiropractic may be in the process of taking place. Psychoanalysis earlier had similarly been broadly accepted into orthodox psychiatry, and homeopathy long since became almost indistinguishable in practice from allopathic medicine.[12] In each of these cases, practitioners either became doctors before taking up the deviant theory or were obliged to undertake a period of training approximating that of orthodox practitioners. The fact that this is less true for chiropractors partly explains the more limited tolerance displayed towards them by contemporary organized American medicine. But the degree of tolerance orthodox medicine is able to display towards its marginal competitors depends upon the security of its own position. That the consensus regarding the legitimacy of orthodox medicine is much less solid in the United States than in Britain largely explains why organized medicine in the latter country has tended to be more tolerant of marginal practitioners than it has in the United States. Moreover, of course, the competitive situation of marginal medicine in America has always been more viable than it has in the United Kingdom. Medical care provided free for the mass of the population in Britain ensures an almost complete orthodox monopoly of service for virtually all illnesses, except psychological or chronic physical illness, for which effective remedies are unavailable.

The fact that a process of absorption of marginal into orthodox medicine is possible, however, can be the source of tensions within a marginal medical group. Chiropractic, osteopathy and Dianetics all experienced strains between the 'straights' who wished to maintain their practice independent of, and untainted by, compromise with orthodox medicine, and the 'mixers' who were willing to compromise, and sought eclectically to combine components of the theory and technique of both systems.

The papers presented in this volume explore various aspects of the nature, development and clientele of marginal medicine. John Lee, in Chapter 2, discusses the changes which have taken place in the social and medical climate, giving rise to new forms of marginal medical practice. Arthur Nudelman in Chapter 3 addresses the issue of how a non-scientific system of therapeutic enterprise is able to maintain itself in an environment which would appear to be increasingly hostile towards the ideas on which it is based. Walter Wardwell presents an analytic scheme for distinguishing orthodox and unorthodox practitioners in Chaper 4, and discusses the changes currently underway in the relationship between the proponents of one marginal medical system, chiropractic, and those of orthodox medicine. In Chapters 5 and 6, Wallis, and Allen and Wallis, analyse two marginal medical collectivities. Dianetics was a short-lived, psychotherapeutically-based system which professed to be able to cure a large part of man's ills on the ground that these stemmed from psychological experiences, notably traumatic experiences of intra-uterine life. Dianetics later developed into a religious-philosophical system, Scientology. Pentecostalists have almost always believed that God can heal by direct or indirect intervention. The paper by Allen and Wallis explores the range of justifications for illness and theories of its alleviation held by the members of a particular pentecostal church, and their utilization of orthodox and pentecostal healing. Finally, Roebuck and Quan, in Chapter 7, analyse the responses of lower-income black and white inhabitants of a town in the southern United States and explore the differences in their utilization of orthodox and unorthodox medical resources.

NOTES AND REFERENCES

1   Emile Durkheim, *The Division of Labour,* Free Press, New York, 1964.
2   E. S. Turner, *Call The Doctor: A Social History of Medical Men,* Michael Joseph, London, 1958, p. 27.

3   T. H. Marshall, *Citizenship and Social Class*, Cambridge University Press, London, 1950.

4   Terence J. Johnson, *Professions and Power,* Macmillan, London, 1972, p. 43.

5   Ibid.

6   A. M. Carr-Saunders and P. M. Wilson, *The Professions,* Clarendon Press, Oxford, 1933, p. 88.

7   Philip Elliott, *The Sociology of the Professions,* Herder & Herder, New York, 1972, p. 37.

8   Rodney M. Coe, *Sociology of Medicine,* McGraw Hill, New York, 1970, p. 194.

9   Richard Harrison Shryock, *The Development of Modern Medicine,* Gollancz, London, 1948.

10   Louis S. Reed, *The Healing Cults*, University of Chicago Press, Chicago, 1932, pp. 3-4.

11   Walter I. Wardwell, 'Limited, Marginal and Quasi-practitioners' in Howard Freeman, Sol Levine, and Leo G. Reeder (eds.), *Handbook of Medical Sociology*, Prentice-Hall, New Jersey, 1963.

12   Walter I. Wardwell, 'Orthodoxy and heterodoxy in medical practice', *Social Science and Medicine*, Vol. 6, 1972, pp. 759-763.

PART ONE:

MEDICAL CHANGE AND SOCIAL CHANGE

John A. Lee

2

Social Change and Marginal Therapeutic Systems

Health has long been defined by humanity in broader terms than physical well-being. The relationship of the body's fitness to the condition of the spirit or psyche was understood by tribal societies and ancient civilizations. The primitive shaman was both a religious functionary and a practical healer, tracing misfortune as well as illness to the malign action of spirits.[1]

Holiness and health have the same etymological root, reflecting the ancient conviction that well-being and right relationship with deity go hand in hand.[2] Old Testament authors regarded sickness and injury as part of the condition of sin.[3] Puritans associated sickness with laziness and a lack of 'self control'.[4] Samuel Butler took the immorality of illness to its logical extreme in *Erewhon*. There are still those who believe it is somehow wrong to be unwell, and who suspect malingering in every delayed recovery. Some find it embarrassing to take the sick role, and protect the activity of this role in backstage areas.[5]

But the thrust of modern secular-scientific medicine has been in the opposite direction. It holds that illness is basically the result of mechanical failure rather than spiritual shortcoming. This failure is seen as precipitated by alien agents which know nothing of the patient's sins or virtues. Germs and viruses are at fault, not people. Health is a matter of nutrition, sanitation, immunization, antisepsis – not a matter of penitence and righteousness. Material therapy is the essence of modern medicine, whether in radiation treatment, antibiotics or transplants. It is not so much that the psyche is denied, but that it is conveniently ignored. The spirit is short-circuited by lancet or tranquillizer.

For many centuries, the practice of healing involved manipulation both of the body and the psyche, although the practitioners of religious and occult healing may not accept a 'scientific' explanation that the efficacy of their treatments is often due to the 'power of suggestion'. These healers attribute their power to other sources: God's Divine Mind, the Thetan, Life Force, the Innate, spirits, and so forth.

The early temple practice of Egypt and Greece involved healing of both material and suggestive kinds. About two hundred temples of Aesculapius were the centres of guilds of priestly physicians.[6] Temples were usually located on mountains and in other places favourable to health. Patients slept in the temple precincts, while priests whispered suggestions in their ears.

As industry and commerce developed in Egypt's urban centres, the noble and merchant classes could afford personal medical care. They provided a market for independent practitioners free from temple control. The treatment of well-understood and curable disorders became secularized, using mechanical and herbal procedures. The temple was happily left to treat inexplicable disorders by reliance on religious suggestion.

In ancient Greece the same division of labour brought a schism at Cos, where Hippocrates and his colleagues wrote works on medical treatment which ignored the supernatural. Clinical observation and experience became the measure of reliable therapy.

The rise of the Christian religion and the decline in secular knowledge in the Dark Ages brought a return to superstition and religious suggestion. Jesus's emphasis on healing as a valid religious activity was exaggerated to the point of excessive veneration of saintly relics. The power of suggestion to obtain cures is demonstrated by the discrediting of some of these relics in recent times. The bones of St Paul at Palermo, for example, proved to be those of a goat.[7]

Lay physicians were profoundly distrusted as likely atheists and grave-robbers, since the chuch forbade autopsy.[8] Mental illness and many physical misfortunes were attributed to witchcraft. Even Renaissance reformers like Paracelsus retained demonological explanations of disease.[9] When Vesalius published his treatise on anatomy, his students were persecuted by Catholic and Calvinist alike. Christian theology insisted on the fallen state of the human body, 'born between piss and feces' (St Augustine). This ideological posture made it more likely that physicians concerned with physical well-being would reject any serious emphasis on spiritual health.

It was not until the nineteenth century that biology began to provide medicine with an empirical basis for a secular, materialist approach to healing. Physicians were no longer likely to be clerics, even in the eighteenth century, but they were honoured more for their style as courtiers and gentlemen, than for their abilities in the surgery. Though a spirit of 'scientific medicine' was abroad, the great majority of medical prescriptions had no significant pharmacological effect. Suggestion (or the placebo effect) still played a vital role prior to 1850.[10]

It was the bacteriology of Bassi (1835), Schonlein (1839), Henle (1840), and most important, Pasteur, which laid the foundations of modern *materia medica*. Concern for the general psychic condition of the patient was overshadowed by the simple pragmatism of the 'germ theory of disease'.

Allopathy and Homeopathy

Today allopathy and medicine are virtually synonymous, but this was not always the case. When Dr Samuel Hahnemann proposed homeopathy as a scientific approach to healing in the late eighteenth century, it seemed at least as reasonable. Homeopathy seeks to 'treat like with like' (Greek, *homoios*: like; *pathos*: suffering). Attenuated drugs were given to induce symptoms similar to those of the disorder suffered. In contrast, allopathy (*allos*: other) attempts to induce a condition incompatible with the disorder. The homeopath induces fever to fight fever, the allopath cools the patient.

The difference is more than one of technique. Indeed, allopathy may adopt homeopathic techniques. Vaccination is a familiar example. Homeopathy seeks to treat the patient rather than the disease. Thus treatment must vary more, patient by patient, than in allopathy. Pasteur's discovery of germs provided a simple and reliable means for treating all patients, largely disregarding individual differences. The allopathic physician is more concerned to isolate and identify the offending bacteria, find a counteracting agent, and administer it. The eventual goal is to eliminate the germ entirely. Homeopathy, by contrast, sees 'germs' as an essential part of the human equilibrium with the natural environment. Since even the most fearful plagues do not destroy the whole population, it seems important to examine not only the germ, but also the 'terrain' (or what modern biology would call the 'ecosystem') in which the disease occurs. Many persons carry tuberculosis bacilli without developing TB.[11]

During Pasteur's lifetime, the respected physiologist Claude Bernard provided a scientific explanation for homeopathy. He theorized that the human body possesses a 'homeostatic facility' which operates to maintain health, and which he saw not as absence of germs or disease, but as equilibrium between organism and environment. While the allopath regards disease as a breakdown to be repaired, the homeopath sees it as evidence of the body's efforts to heal itself. Though Pasteur conceded on his deathbed, 'Bernard is right, the microbe is nothing, the terrain is everything,'[12] the public pressure for immediate improvements in health care has steadily pushed medical practitioners to favour allopathy: find and destroy the offending bacteria or virus.

'But personality is not a pablum for the growth of germs or a stony citadel for their repulsion,' argues Dr Arthur Guirdham.[13] 'It is something which at times admits the invasion of microbes not solely because of their strength and number but to solve problems of strain and mental conflict.' It follows that methods of healing which work on the personality to strengthen its resistance to invasion, might be as fruitful as antiseptics, vaccines and antibiotics. We might look to psychology to provide such defensive measures, but modern psychology has largely adopted the same mechanistic approach as allopathic medicine. Intangibles of 'suggestion' are largely ignored by experimental psychology. Or worse, they are rejected as 'hypnotism' or 'Mesmerism'.

Therapeutic Suggestion

Hypnosis is simply a condition of increased suggestibility. Suggestion is the process of introducing an idea into a person's mind and bringing about its acceptance without the use of critical argument or rational persuasion. Suggestibility is the degree of readiness and capability of an individual to accept a suggestion (i.e. suggested idea).[14]

There is nothing more mysterious to it than that. Hypnosis is not a black art practised by Svengalis and Mandrakes. In its milder forms it has been an integral part of religion since worship began. There is an element of suggestion in every healing art. The physician must inspire confidence through a reassuring 'bedside manner', and may use more direct suggestive manipulation by prescribing a placebo.[15]

Franz Anton Mesmer was the first to propose a naturalistic, secular theory of suggestion, though he called it 'animal magnetism'. Unlike religious healing, his practice did not depend on the saintliness of the healer or the faith of the sufferer. Mesmer's patients sat in a circle around a large tub of iron filings, each holding a rod projecting from the tub. Mesmer and his assistants generated a mood of credibility and expectancy which often led to demonstrable healing.

A commission of scientists appointed by the French government to study Mesmer's healings did not deny that he had somehow effected 'cures'. They attributed the cures to the 'workings of the patients' imaginations' rather than to the healing tub. The failure of the investigators to recognize that cures achieved by 'imagination' were of equal scientific interest to those achieved by other means, led to the branding of Mesmer as a charlatan. The highly credulous or suggestible state into which he manipulated his patients became known as 'being mesmerized'.

In 1841 a Manchester physician, James Braid, investigated the condition resembling sleep which he was able to induce in patients, and invented the word 'hypnosis' (Greek, *hypnos*: sleep). It was not until 1882 that the French Academy of Medicine recognized the medical uses of suggestion. British, American and Canadian medicine waited until the mid-twentieth century. In 1958 the American Medical Association recognized 'a significant place for hypnosis in modern medical practice', but a survey five years later showed that less than 4 per cent of physicians used it.[16] A Toronto survey in 1967 found only 3 per cent trained in hypnosis.[17]

Thus the knowledge of suggestive therapy existed from the eighteenth century onwards, but medical practitioners left the field wide open for other types of healers. At the same time, the great breakthroughs in medicine by Lister, Pasteur and others created a new expectation that science could defeat most pain and disease. Yet it was a long time before the new medicine reached the common multitudes. Major killers such as diptheria, tuberculosis, pneumonia and scarlet fever were not brought under control, especially in the lower social classes, until the twentieth century.[18]

Secular applications of suggestion had been discredited as 'mesmerism' but the way was open for a new form of *religious* suggestive therapy. The incentive was also present, since traditional religious world-views were crumbling before the advance of science. Though orthodox religions had won the first battles with astronomy, anatomy and geology in earlier centuries, their war with science was now certainly lost. The natural sciences were inspiring the same devotion and hope which previous generations had accorded religion.

Out of these social conditions emerged a new variety of religion, appealing to the public yearning for health and well-being. It offered a short-cut to resolve the disappointment with medicine's slow practical achievements, while simultaneously presenting its ideology as a 'new science', thus assuring popularity.

New Thought

The most influential example of this new religious thought occurred in New England in the United States, and began as New Thought. It was a hybrid of Transcendentalism, American 'manifest destiny', and Horatio Alger-type optimism about the possibilities of self-improvement. Its chief tenets were

    a. The omnipotence of God, not as remote sovereign but as

omnipresent source of power or energy.

b. The divinity of man and thus his God-given right to tap the divine power.

c. The unreality of matter (only Idea is real).

d. The unlimited capacity of the human mind when correctly attuned to God's power.

The outcomes of this curious variant of Christianity are numerous, ranging from Norman Vincent Peale's 'power of positive thinking' to Mary Baker Eddy's 'Christian Science' – to say nothing of secular manifestations such as Dale Carnegie's *How to Win Friends and Influence People*. The contemporary literature of New Thought fills whole shelves in many American bookstores, and offers readers the means to 'think themselves' into happiness, riches, fame and power.

The aspect of New Thought with which we are concerned here is that dealing with the problem of injury and pain. Although matter might be overruled and even abolished by mind, the human experience of disease, disorder and death remained apparently real. The New Thought solution lay in 'apparently'. These were *seeming* afflictions, illusions, mistaken thoughts.[19]

Mind Cure

The appropriate treatment of illusory pain is 'mind cure'. Its practice is attractively simple, that of auto-suggestion. This should not be confused with Victorian 'will power', 'mind over matter', or Couéism. The mind-cure practitioner does not tell himself to 'buck up', 'keep a stiff upper lip' or 'bear with it'. Nor does he optimistically and self-deceptively argue that there is less pain today than yesterday, so that 'every day in every way I am growing better and better'. Such elementary formulas would be dismissed as merely 'kidding oneself'.

Mind cure is a more radical solution, striking at the experiential roots of pain in the mind itself. Its most convincing exponent was Mary Baker Eddy, founder of Christian Science. She repeatedly warned that will power is not the answer.[20] Instead, the practi-

tioner must deny the very existence of pain. Disease, injury, pain
are all illusions, misapprehensions, mistaken thoughts.

To demonstrate her argument, Mrs Eddy cited numerous
familiar instances of pains which exist only in mistaken thought:
for example, the pain experienced in the hand of a person who has
had his arm amputated years before.[21] Mrs Eddy did not discount
the power of illusions to affect our behaviour, whether they be real
or not. The mirage in the desert, the apparently bent stick in water,
can certainly influence our behaviour. Indeed, she recognized the
positive power of 'malicious animal magnetism' to corrupt our
thinking.[22] But once the practitioner *knows* that an illusion is only
that, then it can no longer influence behaviour. Thus it is the act of
knowing, rather than will, which leads to well-being.[23]

Obviously Mrs Eddy distinguished her religious doctrine from
'so-called mind cure' which, she argued, had its 'birth in Mortal
Mind' rather than in Divine Mind.[24] She also rejected the
argument that her methods were those of self-hypnosis or auto-
suggestion.[25]

Yet throughout her writings there is a constant preoccupation
with the problem of exposure to 'bad suggestions'. Aside from her
charge that these were being deliberately directed against her by
enemies,[26] Mrs Eddy warns her followers not to expose themselves
to ideas of pain and disease, as these will only mislead them.
Believers should not study anatomy, or even hygiene.[27] Indeed,
they should not even record their ages, as death too is an illusion.[28]
The healthy person will act as constant 'gatekeeper of the mind' to
keep out the most random thoughts of illness.[29]

Donald Meyer has examined in detail the social origins of mind
cure, positive thinking and Christian Science, and his work need
not be summarized here.[30] However, it is interesting to note that
mind cure provided a new social role for would-be healers, with
advantages not available to those pursuing the profession of medicine. The disadvantages of 'faith healing' and even less reputable
healing roles (quacks, witches, etc.) were nicely avoided. The
mind-cure practitioner claimed the distinction of *science* – and
made sure to substantiate this by ample reference to scientific
example, as well as by the use of scientific language.

The mind-cure practitioner did not spend long and difficult years acquiring medical skills and knowledge. He or she could step into the admired social role of healer immediately. The role strain of keeping up with the headlong rush of medical discovery – the latest in drugs, techniques, diagnosis – could also be avoided. Mind-cure technique, once understood, is an eternal, unchanging and beautifully simple Truth.

The emergence of mind cure coincided with the first generation of generally literate Americans, graduates of the new public schools open to even the lower classes. Reading is an exhilarating experience for the newly literate. It becomes possible to travel to distant worlds and times, and to share the thoughts of countless men and women. Reading played a special role in the development of mind cure. Every reader was invited to cure himself of injury or disease by earnest reading of mind-cure books. Numerous cures are still attributed, for example, to a single careful reading of Mrs Eddy's book *Science and Health*.[31]

Spiritualist Healing

Spiritualist healing is probably more familiar than Christian Science to English readers, due to the fame of one of its leading practitioners, Harry Edwards. Its origins are ancient, but spiritualism emerged in its *modern* form at almost the same time as Christian Science, and in the same social milieu – New York State in the 1850s. Moreover, like Christian Science and many other expressions of New Thought, its original impetus came from women.[32]

Spiritualist healing is based on the beliefs that:

a. Individuals continue after death in disembodied form, as spirits.
b. Some humans, called *mediums*, are able to communicate with these spirits, and to apply their powers in the living world.
c. At least some spirits, called *guides*, are concerned for the health of living persons and willing to provide their healing services via a medium.

   d. Thought is closer to spirit than matter, and it is important
      for well-being to have positive thoughts. Healers may treat
      by thought alone when necessary, *'in absentia'*.

Spiritualism differs from Christian Science in that, rather than
denying outright the existence of a material world, it postulates a
co-existent but more fundamental world of the spirit, in which
things are made up of 'astral energy' and 'ectoplasm'. The task of
the healer is to direct astral energy (often by the movement of the
hands, as well as by positive thought), under the guidance of the
healing spirit. Mrs Eddy began her healing with similar hand
movements, but later abandoned them in favour of exclusively
mental healing. Logically enough, spiritual healers often believe
they are specially gifted in curing certain diseases, according to the
fame of their spirit guide when he was alive.[33]

Spiritualist healing relies much less on suggestion through
printed material than does Christian Science. This reflects the
social class of its followers, at least in Canada. Christian Scientists
are likely to be business and professional people, well educated and
highly literate, while spiritualists are more likely to be working
class people.

Unity Church of Truth

Unity is closely related to Christian Science in origin and doctrine,
and like Christian Science and spiritualist healing, is primarily the
practice of women. Mrs Fillmore, a key founder, was healed after
contact with Christian Science in 1887, but rather than affiliate
with Mrs Eddy's church, she joined with her husband to found
Unity.

Unity emphasizes the importance of controlled thought and the
avoidance of any suggestion of illness. Diseases should not be
named in thought.[34] Healing takes place through careful study of
Unity's numerous publications, together with prayer. 'Deny the
matter and material conditions,' a Unity handbook urges, prom-
ising that numerous disorders, including syphilis, can be cured by
'profound realization of truth'.[35] Even epidemics can be repudi-

ated by 'quietly, confidently, peacefully knowing' their unreality, a doctrine very similar to that of Mrs Eddy.[36]

Twentieth-Century Mind Cure

Perhaps the most colourful outgrowth of New Thought is 'Dianetics', the 'modern science of mental health' invented by L. Ron Hubbard in 1950. This practice began as the discovery of 'the hidden source of all psychosomatic ills and human aberration' and offered the skills for 'their inevitable cure'.[37] An estimated 70 per cent of 'Man's listed ailments' might be considered psychosomatic.[38]

Hubbard's hidden source was the Reactive Mind, a functional equivalent of Mrs Eddy's Mortal Mind. It played the same role in fouling up man's correct understanding of reality, by recording 'engrams' of painful experience which operated as 'demon circuits' in a manner analagous to Mrs Eddy's 'malicious animal magnetism'. As with *Science and Health*, a single reading of *Dianetics* could produce a practitioner 'more skilled and able to treat the mind than anyone attempting to do so, regardless of reputation, a short time ago'.[39]

Dianetics is now largely of historical interest as the precursor of Scientology, an 'applied religious philosophy' in which emphasis has shifted from healing to 'making able people more able'. However, the doctrinal centrality of the act of *knowing* the unreality of matter (in this case M.E.S.T., or matter, energy, space and time) continues, even in the name Scientology itself (the study of knowing).[40]

Of course Hubbard would probably deny any derivation of Dianetics or Scientology from New Thought, just as, like Mrs Eddy, he denies any application of suggestion or hypnosis. The Dianetic 'reverie' and Scientology auditing were both said to be processes of knowing and controlling the self, rather than the use of suggestion. Yet the specific 'clear procedures' of Scientology involve conditions of increased suggestibility, and may produce effects similar to those of hypnosis.[41]

Scientology emphasizes that it is not in the field of physical healing,[42] but rather is concerned with the improvement of intelligence, with development of personality, and with 'success'.[43] It shares with Psycho-cybernetics, Concept Therapy, Norman Vincent Peale's Positive Thinking, and similar modern versions of New Thought, a preoccupation with increased psychological well-being and power in the practitioner. It also shares with these groups a predilection for scientific terminology and analogy.

The use of apparently scientific devices lends credibility to the claims of modern mind cure, in the eyes of believers. One of the favourite devices is a version of the skin galvanometer. V.G. Mathison developed an 'electropsychometer', which became the basis for his organization of Electropsychometry, which has not survived his death.[44] Analysis of the 'patient' by means of measured responses to a skin galvanometer during an interview, was combined with explicit use of suggestion in 'self-hypno' tapes to be replayed each night before sleep.[45] The 'E-meter' used in Scientology appears to be another example of use of the skin galvanometer to lend a scientific aura to an interview procedure.

Concept Therapy is the invention of a Texan chiropractor, Thurman Fleet, with the assistance of a Methodist faith healer and successful hypnotist, Reverend E. L. Crump. This group is little known outside of chiropractic circles, but has enjoyed some success in converting members of this profession to its brand of mind cure. Again there is emphasis on knowing the unreality of physical disorder, as in Christian Science: 'What is it worth for you to learn how to better defend yourself against thoughts which may cause cancer. . . ?'[46] But the approach is more modern, and is explicit in its use of suggestion, which is taught in courses on hypnosis. While chiropractic manipulation heals the physical body, 'concept therapy' heals the psyche.

Psychotherapeutic Mind Cure

The first half of the twentieth century witnessed great changes in the field of medicine, surpassing even the wildest dreams not only of its own practitioners, but also of healers by mind cure. What Christian Scientist or spiritualist healer has successfully restored a detached limb, or replaced a damaged organ, or eliminated a widespread disease through vaccination or antibiotics?

Out-distanced in physical healing, the advocates of mind cure have turned to the healing of the psyche. Until very recently they were aided in this choice by the preponderance of experimental and behaviourist approaches in psychology. Modern advocates of versions of New Thought have charged psychology with abandoning the human spirit.[47] Their new charge against material medicine is not its failure to deliver the goods for the body, but its inability to heal the minds of anxious and nervous men and women in an urbanized, jet-paced, nuclear-armed world.

Where can the patient go for personal, unhurried consideration of the well-being of his or her 'whole person'? Not to the general practitioner or the psychiatrist. The doctor's office has become something of an assembly line, with patients moving through every five or six minutes. Recently the Ontario government pressured the College of Physicians and Surgeons into setting limits on the number of patients various practitioners could treat per week. The impulse was not therapeutic so much as financial; practitioners were charging the state health care programme for hundreds of patients per week. As a consequence, 'limits' were set.

For example, an Ontario psychiatrist is 'limited' to 155 patient treatment claims per week.[48] At this rate, even with the exclusive use of group therapy, a therapist working eight hours a day, six days a week, could not give direct personal attention to any patient for more than twenty minutes a week. Of course one of the results of these conditions is an upsurge in psychotherapeutic movements of 'encounter', 'sensitivity training', 'anger therapy', 'Gestalt therapy' and even 'poetry therapy'. But the continued growth of religious and pseudo-scientific mind cure groups indicates a considerable unmet need for psychotherapy. 1942146

Some of the need has been met by a revival of religious 'faith healing'. As the orthodox Christian Churches have demythologized their doctrines and rituals, with a consequent depersonalization for the believers, there has been a shift towards the warmer religious experience of fundamentalist sects. However, faith healing has tended to remain concentrated on physical rather than psychical healing, perhaps because the results of physical healing are more obvious and dramatic.

Faith Healing and Mind Cure

It is unlikely that religious faith healing will be able to offer effective and attractive psychotherapeutic services to modern populations. Thus faith healing is likely to remain in competition with material medicine in physical healing – a competition in which religion is likely to lose ground steadily – while modern versions of mind cure, which have switched to psychological methods and objectives, will compete more effectively with 'scientific' medicine.

The reasons lie in fundamental doctrinal differences between faith healing and mind cure. These include:

1   Mind cure assumes an abstract deity in the form of energy or power, which is always accessible to the human mind, if the correct attunement procedure is used. Faith healing postulates a personal and rather arbitrary deity who must be worshipped rather than 'tapped'. This deity may choose, for hidden reasons, to refuse to respond to human initiatives.

2   Mind cure's universe is monistic. Reality is spiritual or psychic, and the material world is at best a temporal expression of spirit (as in spiritualism) or, at worst, a delusion (as in Christian Science). It follows that pain and disease are mistaken thoughts, which correct thought may eliminate. Faith healing assumes a dualistic universe, in which good (God) and evil (Satan) contend for power. Man is not able to correct disorder on his own, as he lives in a fallen world and is himself no longer basically good, but rather, in need of redemption through suffering. Hence pain not only exists; it has its place and purpose in God's plan.

3   Mind cure employs the 'power of suggestion' more effectively than does faith healing. True, there are elements of suggestion in a religious healing meeting, and in the enthusiasm of an Oral Roberts, but there is a greater element of conviction and certainty

in mind cure. Faith healers have to explain failures in terms of an unpredictable deity, or some undefinable unworthiness of the believer. 'God moves in mysterious ways.' The mind-cure practitioner explains failure simply as 'error' with no need to examine either the shortcomings of the believer or the whims of the deity. As with a formula in algebra, if the solution is not forthcoming, some rule of procedure has been ignored. Once the procedure is correct, the solution must follow.

This process of 'having certainty on experience' (as Scientology expresses it, for example) is conducive to greater suggestive or hypnotic impact. The demonstrable effects of suggestion are well known, for example in reducing pain in childbirth.[49] The conviction of the Scientologist that correct procedures must certainly bring about the desired condition is expressed both by Hubbard and a former adherent.[50] In addition, the use of scientific terminology and explanation is more accessible to practitioners of mind cure than to faith healers. Since science probably now enjoys a higher level of pragmatic certainty than does religion, this also adds to the suggestive power of mind cure, in contrast to faith healing. That is, more persons are likely to consult scientific data and procedures in matters of vocation, education, travel, and health – to name but a few examples – than are likely to pray or consult a priest.

CONCLUSION

Mind cure may be understood as a response to certain social and technical conditions in the field of health care, but it has also had an impact, in turn, on the development of medicine. One outcome is the continued fostering of high expectations of well-being among modern populations (in contrast to resignation to illness as a natural or God-willed event). No doubt 'positive thought' about health has contributed to public support for generous allocations of state resources to medical research and public health care. For although Mrs Eddy may have had her doubts about public hygiene, her followers, along with spiritualist healers and others, have been ready to urge public support of such services – for example by workmen's compensation boards and insurance companies.[51]

More important, mind cure (more so than faith healing) has kept alive the homeopathic tradition in healing. By emphasis on the well-being of the psyche or spirit, and the condition of health as wholeness of the person, mind cure and its modern derivatives have served as a countervailing social force to the main drift of modern medicine towards mechanical and chemical treatments.

It is less rare today than several decades ago to find patients who demand a careful explanation of the reasons for prescription of a certain drug or procedure. I find among younger doctors in Ontario an increasing willingness to respond to patients' scepticism. Instead of meekly following 'doctor's orders' patients are often taking the attitude 'It's my body, after all', and more physicians are agreeing. The insistence of positive thought on the importance of the patient's mental attitude to healing as a vital factor, now finds more acceptance in medicine, as psychosomatic phenomena become better understood. Mind cure has kept a door open, through which responses have recently been possible to hypnosis, acupuncture and similar, previously disparaged methods.

One of the most controversial but potentially constructive consequences of continued advocacy of mind cure is the insistence on the right of patients *not to be treated* by 'scientific' medicine. Christian Scientists pioneered in this area, with their refusal to comply with state vaccination laws. They met with derision and abuse for their refusal to surrender to the new god of science. The same sort of detraction is now the lot of Scientology, which has chosen to challenge 'scientific' medicine in the field of mental health.[52]

Scientology publications have actively championed the rights of mental patients.[53] The battle between Scientology – a modern version of mind cure more concerned with psychic than physical well-being – and the psychiatrists promises to re-enact the early campaigns between Christian Scientists and physicians. The implications of this new contest may be judged from the role now being assigned to criminal psychiatry in the Soviet Union. Modern medicine is still sometimes ready to shortcircuit the spirit with lancet and tranquillizer, and mind-cure groups may help to protect us from unhappy consequences.

NOTES AND REFERENCES

1   Jerome D. Frank, *Persuasion and Healing*, Johns Hopkins University Press, Baltimore, 1961, p. 50.

2   Leslie D. Weatherhead, *Psychology, Religion and Healing*, Hodder & Stoughton, London, 1951, p. 31.

3   See, for example, Job 4:7, 'Think now, who that was innocent ever perished?'

4   Donald Meyer, *The Positive Thinkers*, Doubleday Anchor, New York, 1966, p. 43.

5   See Sidney Jourard, 'Healthy Personality and Self Disclosure', *Mental Hygiene*, Vol. 43, 1959.

6   Weatherhead, op. cit., p. 29.

7   United Church of Canada, 'Sickness and Health' (pamphlet), 1965, p. 17.

8   Benjamin Lee Gordon, *The Romance of Medicine,* Davis, New York, 1945, p. 298.

9   Ibid., p. 178.

10   A. K. Shapiro, 'The placebo effect in the history of medical treatment', *American Journal of Psychiatry*, Vol. 116, 1959, pp. 298-304.

11   Brian Inglis, *Fringe Medicine*, Faber & Faber, London, 1964, p. 91.

12   Ibid., p. 140. Hans Selye is a modern advocate of the homeostatic concept.

13   Arthur Guirdham, *Disease and the Social System*, Allen & Unwin, London, 1942, p. xi.

14   A. M. Weitzenhoffer, *General Techniques of Hypnotism*, Grune & Stratton, New York, 1957, p. 32.

15   See Frank, op. cit., p. 70: 'an average of 55% [of patients] showed significant symptomatic improvement from placebos.'

16   *Medical Economic Magazine* Survey, quoted by Lewis R. Wolberg, *Medical Hypnosis,* Grune & Stratton, New York, 1948, p. 25.

17   John A. Lee, *Sectarian Healers*, Queen's Printers, Toronto, 1970, p. 18.

18   Meyer, op. cit., p. 46.

19   Ibid., pp. 55ff.

20 Mary Baker Eddy, *Science and Health with Key to the Scriptures,* Published by Trustees of the Will of Mrs Eddy, Boston, Mass., p. 206.

21 Ibid., p. 212.

22 See *Church Manual* of the Christian Science Mother Church, article 8, section 8.

23 Eddy, op. cit., pp. 390-412.

24 Ibid., p. 185.

25 Ibid., p. 104.

26 Charles S. Braden, *Christian Science Today,* Southern Methodist University Press, Dallas, Texas, 1958, p. 344.

27 Eddy, op. cit., p. 179, and 1898 edition, p. 381.

28 Ibid., p. 246.

29 Ibid., p. 175.

30 Meyer, op. cit.

31 See Eddy, op. cit., 'Fruitage', Chapter XVIII, pp. 601ff; also most current issues of the *Journal* of Christian Science.

32 The Fox sisters, Margaret, Catherine and Leah, at Hydeville, New York, in 1848. Most modern mediums are women.

33 Reports by spiritualist healers in Toronto, Canada. See John A. Lee, op. cit., pp. 104-117.

34 T. D. Schobert, *Divine Remedies,* Unity, Lee's Summit, Missouri, 1965, Foreword.

35 Ibid., p. 50.

36 Clara Palmer, *You Can be Healed,* Unity, Lee's Summit, Missouri, 1959, p. 182.

37 L. Ron Hubbard, *Dianetics, The Modern Science of Mental Health,* Hubbard College of Scientology, East Grinstead, Sussex; quoted from the dustjacket of the edition sold by Toronto Scientology in 1967, but since revised to exclude this claim.

38 'The Scope of Scientology, the Need to Change', in *Scientology Newsletter,* 1965: 'Of what must a science of mind be composed? . . . (Item 6). The cause and cure of all psychosomatic ills, which number, some say, 70% of Man's listed ailments.'

39 Hubbard, op. cit., p. 167 (1967 version).

40 L. Ron Hubbard, *Dianetics 55!,* Grant Production Ltd., London, 1961, pp. 67ff; pp. 153ff; see also *Clear News,* Advanced Organization Los Angeles, No. 21, 10 April, 1970; and *Advance* No. 10, Church of Scientology of California, 1970, p. 10, in which 'Kay Romeao, OT VII' reports an exteriorization experience: 'It was 2 am. The body was asleep. I was exterior and very much aware, I received the intention of someone praying for help. I went there and saw a murder about to be committed. As a thetan exterior, with intention I stopped the murder. Then, with the body, had someone call the police.'

41   L. Ron Hubbard, *Clear Procedure,* Hubbard College of Scientology, 1957, pp. 18ff; *Dianetics 55!,* op. cit., p. 124.

42   *Clear Procedure,* p. 7. However, note that in 1967 Hubbard was still presenting theory on treatment, e.g., p. 15 of *Scientology, The Fundamentals of Thought,* 1967 edition, Church of Scientology, Washington, (American International Printing).

43   L. Ron Hubbard, 'What it means to be a Scientologist', *The Auditor,* No. 36: 'Scientology, for the first time in Man's history, can predictably raise intelligence.'

44   Lee, op. cit., pp. 91ff.

45   Ibid.

46   William Wolfe, *Psychic Self Improvement for the Millions,* Sherbourne Press, Los Angeles, 1966, p. 23.

47   Hubbard, 'What it means . . .', op. cit.: 'Psyche is Greek for spirit. But modern psychology has nothing to do with the mind or the spirit. . . . Wundt in Leipzig, Germany in 1879. He's the only authority for modern psychology. . . .'

48   *Toronto Daily Star,* 11 June, 1973, p. 1.

49   Weatherhead, op. cit., provides some startling examples, including hypnotic control of body temperature from 96 to 104 degrees, though body temperature is generally considered involuntary, p. 122.

50   Robert Kaufman, *Inside Scientology,* Olympia Press, New York, 1972, pp. 145ff; L. Ron Hubbard, *Clear Procedure,* op. cit., pp. 16ff and 'Theory of Training in Scientology', *The Auditor,* No. 37.

51   Lee, op. cit., Appendix II.

52   See *Psychology Today,* October 1974: 'Field Report; Civil Rights and the Mentally Ill'.

53   *Freedom,* Church of Scientology of Toronto, undated issue in 1971, p. 2, compares death rates in war and mental hospitals (the latter being higher), and p. 3: 'There is no corruption quite like psychiatric corruption.' *Freedom,* Church of Scientology of California, January 1975, devotes pp. 3, 5 and 8 to critiques of shock treatment and a 'cover-up' of a patient's death in St. Louis, Missouri, State Mental Hospital.

Arthur E. Nudelman

3

The Maintenance of Christian Science in Scientific Society

The continued existence of Christian Science, a religion known primarily for its teachings regarding health, illness and healing, is perplexing to many persons of other faiths. Although many people turn to a deity for assistance in overcoming illness, few believe that a person can preserve health and combat illness simply by attuning himself to the Christian Scientific Truth that sickness and pain are based entirely on 'suggestion'[1] and exist only in the errant beliefs of men. Mary Baker Eddy, the founder of Christian Science, wrote: 'That which [God] creates is good, and He makes all that is made. Therefore the only reality of sin, sickness, or death is the awful fact that unrealities seem real to human, erring belief, until God strips off their disguise.'[2]

The primary purpose of this report is to examine how Christian Science has managed to survive in increasingly secular societies, especially in the United States of America, where frequent medical advances are widely publicized and where, both *per capita* and *in toto*, a greater amount of money is spent on medical services than in any other society in the world. A concluding note will focus on the present status and prospects of Christian Science.

Other writers have dealt with the manner in which deviant beliefs are maintained in the face of exposure to conflicting ideas, derision, and disconfirmed prophesies.[3] Although informed by these reports, the present discussion necessarily differs from them; Christian Science is, after all, a 'respectable' and behaviourally unemotional religion with a middle-class membership, not a lower-class cult such as those most commonly studied by social scientists

42

interested in unusual religious beliefs and practices.

This report is based in part on Christian Science literature,[4] reports of social scientists and historians,[5] and conversations with mainstream health personnel, but it is unique in that it also draws on an empirical study of rank-and-file Christian Scientists.

Eighty-five per cent of the undergraduate students who listed their religious preference as 'Christian Science' in a religious census conducted at a large, state-supported American university were interviewed during the 1966-7 academic year. Five converts were dropped from the working sample, leaving a total of forty-eight students ranging from 17 to 23. Twenty-eight of the students were females. The interviews, which lasted approximately an hour and were taped and transcribed, provide information on, among other topics, the structure of religiosity,[6] adaptation to a college environment,[7] conceptions of etiology and treatment of illness,[8] and health and illness behaviour.[9]

This report is divided into five sections, the first four of which concern factors relevant to the maintainance of the sect: (1) beneficial effects of Christian Science, (2) institutionalized concessions to reality, (3) individual behaviour and beliefs, and (4) behaviour and beliefs of the larger society. The final section deals with the sect's current status and prospects.

Beneficial Effects of Christian Science

It is undeniable that many ailments are caused in whole or in part by mental states,[10] and placebos may be effective in remitting such ailments. The effectiveness of medical and religious placebos alike rests on the patient's expectation that he will be helped, and although most Christian Scientists have little confidence in medicine,[11] many have great confidence in their religion.

The effectiveness of religious healing is based on the personal charisma of the healer and/or his or the sect's ideology.[12] In Christian Science, the latter element is most important; with devotion and practice, any Christian Scientist is alleged to be competent to heal himself. A Scientist may, however, enlist the assistance of a Christian Science practitioner,[13] whose healing practice is licensed by the world headquarters of the sect, The Mother Church, in Boston, Massachusetts.

An important factor in Christian Science healing is the type of interaction between practitioner and patient. Jaffe and Slote[14] demonstrated the role of physicians' comments in influencing feelings of well-being or discomfort among hospitalized non-Scientists, and Mrs Eddy's reference to iatrogenic ailments indicates her awareness of the role of suggestion in the etiology and aggravation of illness: 'The ordinary practitioner, examining bodily symptoms, telling the patient that he is sick, and treating the case according to his physical diagnosis, would naturally induce the very disease he is trying to cure, even if it were not already determined by mortal mind.'[15] Christian Science practitioners may or may not understand fully the importance of suggestion in healing, but they do know that dwelling on one's illness may aggravate it. One student said: 'As my practitioner would say: "Well, tell me the good news." Well, how was I supposed to think anything destructive in myself if I [told] her the good news? . . . I had to think positively!'

Even when serious pathology of a type not amenable to placebo treatment is involved, any religion may have a strong palliative effect.[16] Christian Scientists know that as long as man is on this earth, he will be confronted with illusory ailments. But one can tolerate some disability and pain, for these are challenges that, when successfully met, allegedly enable him to grow in his understanding of Science. And a devout Scientist knows that full recovery is imminent if, through study and contemplation, he achieves a realization of the illusory nature of his affliction.

Another beneficial aspect of Christian Science is its satisfying philosophy:[17] goodness abounds; evil, sin, sickness and death are illusory. As a rather unreligious student remarked: 'Christian Science is a beautiful religion.' And to the extent that the Scientific philosophy enables adherents to keep their minds off their problems, they may be relatively unsusceptible to hypochondriasis. Even Scientists who are inept in the utilization of their faith can achieve at least some comfort and peace of mind from the doctrine that God would not create a less-than-perfect man or an evil world, and any ideology that promotes peace of mind is providing a valuable sevice indeed.

In sum, Christian Science can, at least in many cases, contribute to physical and emotional health.[18]

Institutionalized Concessions to Reality

Although the Scientific belief system is painfully challenged by reality at times, this occurs far less frequently than an observer might be led to expect from a perusal of Mrs Eddy's writings. One explanation of how this type of confrontation is kept within tolerable bounds is that Christian Science has – intentionally or unintentionally – made some concessions to physical and biological reality.

Scientists are encouraged to rely on their religion when confronted with physical problems of any nature, but despite Mrs Eddy's contention that all maladies are amenable to Scientific healing, she believed that a Scientist may legitimately consult a physician for certain problems.[19] Just as one takes a malfunctioning automobile to an automotive mechanic for repair, so he may take a malfunctioning human body to a mechanic who specializes in this line of work if he has a 'mechanical problem', which includes surgical cases, fractures, dislocations, and many dental and ocular cases.

Fortunately, mechanical problems tend to be *visible* and visible problems are often *mechanical.* One who has a fracture, an impacted wisdom tooth, or poor eyesight, is generally quite aware that he has a problem. Infectious diseases are serious, but their severity is often not *immediately* apparent. Mechanical problems frequently heal satisfactorily only with professional medical attention, but many other ailments remit spontaneously after they have run their course. This is especially true of that most frequent illness, the 'common cold', for which a physician can be of little assistance. Therefore, when confronted with problems whose visibility and consequences preclude denial of their existence, Scientists usually may legitimately consult a physician. Less obvious problems may ultimately terminate in death or permanent disability, but this occurs more frequently relatively late in life, when one is expected to have physical problems; that the elderly experience poor health is almost, to use a Scientific phrase, a 'universal belief'. Even Mrs Eddy passed on.

Second, discretion is the better part of valour for Scientists as well as non-Scientists. Mrs Eddy stated that 'one should not tarry in the storm if the body is freezing, nor should he remain in the devouring flames. Until one is able to prevent bad results, he should avoid their occasion.' [20] Thus, although 'food does not affect the absolute Life of man,' Scientists continue to eat, for 'it would be foolish to stop eating until we gain perfection and a clear comprehension of the living Spirit.'[21] Scientists also drink water, sleep, wear protective clothing, and study for examinations. As a student said about brushing one's teeth, having a diseased appendix removed, and similar health and illness behaviours, one does not 'stand in the middle of a highway!'

Third, since illness is a fact of life one is often unable to fulfil obligations ranging from washing dishes to going to work and attending classes. Un-Scientific though it may appear to be, Scientists often seek release from role obligations when they sense that they are victims of a 'claim' [22] – that is, when they are not feeling well – and they generally do so with little or no sense of shame.[23] (They would, of course, be expected to refrain from complaining vociferously about their problems.) Illness may be illusory, but a Scientific version of the sick role is very real.

Fourth, Christian Science has adapted in significant ways to a changing world. Mrs Eddy contended that *Science and Health*, the Christian Science textbook, 'contains the complete Science of Mind-healing',[24] and she directed that her *Manual of The Mother Church* 'shall not be revised without the written consent of its author'.[25] Were she alive today, she would probably revise her works; both *Science and Health* and the *Manual* went through a large number of editions during their author's lifetime.[26]

Despite forces acting to maintain Christian Science in its pristine state, it appears that a number of changes have occurred, including a few minor changes in *Science and Health* by the Board of Directors of The Mother Church.[27] Most changes, however, have been accomplished by interpretation, a practice that Braden[28] believes the Board engages in occasionally. And some regulations appear almost universally to be disregarded. For example, Scientists are prohibited from seeking membership in organizations that are not listed in the *Manual*,[29] but were this rule followed, Scientists would not be found in professional societies, college fraternities, and other contemporary organizations.

Another prohibited practice is birth control,[30] but many Scientists probably do not abide by Mrs Eddy's rule. Editorials in the *Christian Science Monitor*, an official Church publication, have dealt with the necessity of birth control for limiting the world's expanding population, and at least one editorial appeared to legitimate even 'the pill'.[31] Excluding four persons who came from homes broken by death or divorce, the students studied had a mean of 1.75 siblings, which approximates national figures for families of similar socio-economic status. Of course, this does not prove that the parents employed artificial methods of birth control, but it is apparent that they did not heed the Biblical injunction to 'be fruitful and multiply'.

The writings of Mrs Eddy and the intransigence of Church officials and many practitioners and rank-and-file Scientists have impeded the adaptation of Christian Science to secular society, to be sure.[32] On balance, however, considerable adaptation has occurred, without which the religion probably could not have survived.

Individual Behaviour and Beliefs

This section focuses on principles of psychodynamics, interpersonal relationships, and unintentional health behaviour. The first factor is selective exposure to information. Scientists are encouraged to avoid unhealthful reports and conversations; in Mrs Eddy's words, 'so long as you read medical works you will be sick'.[33] That is, suggestion can cause illness. Scientists generally do avoid medical reports, accounts of gruesome accidents, etc., preferring to read more 'wholesome' materials such as the *Christian Science Monitor*. Nor do Scientists often select occupations or college

majors that conflict greatly with salient tenets of their faith. One
such area, of course, is the biological sciences. Another is the
behavioural sciences, the deterministic assumptions of which are
also anathema to Scientists.[34] Avoidance of unwholesome reports
and certain academic courses rests both on Mrs Eddy's admon-
itions and, perhaps more importantly, on principles of psychodynamics. Materials that conflict with Christian Science would be
expected to be dissonance-provoking to Scientists.[35]

Since Scientists avoid a good deal of mental contamination from
the biological sciences, they are seldom confronted with un- or
anti-Scientific facts in this realm. For example, some Scientists are
unaware of or sceptical of the etiological significance of micro-
organisms,[36] and probably very few are familiar with Wilson's
findings that the average longevity of Scientists in King County,
Washington was very slightly lower than the average longevity of
the non-Scientist population.[37]

But despite Mrs Eddy's contention that 'there is no physical
science, inasmuch as all truth proceeds from the divine Mind',[38]
50 per cent of the twelve male upperclassmen in the sample had
elected to major in engineering or a basic physical science; in contrast, only 29 per cent of the male non-Scientists at the university
had selected such a major.[39] That Scientists frequently do not
avoid physical science courses and communications dealing with
inanimate objects and phenomena is functional for the survival of
the sect. In general, physical realities are less subject to denial and
systematic distortion than are biological and behavioural phenomena. One can see gravity at work and one sometimes experiences the consequences of failure to keep one's automobile fueled;
but one cannot see one's heart, and the failure of physicians and
drugs to cure the 'common cold' is obvious to Scientists and non-
Scientists alike. And Scientists are not alone in their deprecation of
the deterministic assumptions inherent in the behavioural sciences.
These assumptions and, indeed, often the value of behavioural
science are questioned by persons of many faiths, thus providing
consensual support for the Scientific viewpoint.[40]

Second, although many Scientists do not eschew study of the
physical sciences, the possibility of conflict is present.[41] Coping

mechanisms, the most important of which appears to be compart-mentalization, enable Scientists to meet this conflict. One student, for example, said that 'the physical world and the mental world are two separate things. I don't see how you can possibly try to mix them.' Another said that 'science in the material world is necessary for the existence of the material world. . . . And then my religion is for the way I think about life.'

Third, Christian Science resembles many other belief systems in that to a true believer it cannot be disproved. Mrs Eddy asserted that *Science and Health* contains 'no contradictory statements – at least none which are apparent to those who understand its propositions well enough to pass judgment upon them',[42] and she declared that a practitioner who fails to heal a patient has not lived a Scientific life.[43] Many Scientists follow in her footsteps. Although students were almost unanimous in declaring that Science can help to protect one's health, nine out of ten also believed that a 'good' Scientist could succumb to illness; two-thirds of these attributed this to relaxing one's vigilance against the bogey-man of suggestion.[44] Further, a number of students regretted their inability to use Science while contending that it *does* work for those who diligently practise it. The carrot of success is dangled in front of Scientists. As one student declared, Christian Science is 'very demanding. . . . You have to use it everyday. I mean, you *really* do. People are happy for it after a while. It's demanding in the beginning stages, I think. When you're really involved in it, it's no longer demanding. It's something you really want to do. And then the demand ceases and the enjoyment really begins.'

Simmons, who studied a small religious sect in the south-eastern United States, is probably right in contending that 'no individual can maintain beliefs when a large amount of contrary evidence is *perceived*.'[45] Scientists are, however, unlikely to perceive much cogent evidence contrary to their beliefs. Not only do they avoid exposure to such evidence, as noted above, but they selectively perceive and evaluate the information that comes their way. A cold that vanishes after troubling a person for two weeks proves that Christian Science works. Recovery of a lost hat or wallet, protection from danger while racing automobiles or climbing mountains, and other occurrences, are interpreted as 'demonstrations' of the efficacy of Science. No matter if one breaks one's arm in a bad fall; without Science one would have broken one's neck. No matter if one is forced into bankruptcy; without Science one would have lost one's health as well as one's money. A student on academic probation even attributed her academic 'success' to Science.

Fourth, Christian Scientists are often brought to the attention of physicians when they are in need of medical attention, thus reducing morbidity and mortality that would prove embarrassing to Scientific doctrine. Research on relationships between cognitive variables on the one hand, and health and illness behaviour on the other,[46] suggests that Scientists would be expected to manifest little effective health and illness behaviour of a secular nature. Devout Scientists generally do not believe that they are susceptible to serious illness if they conscientiously apply themselves to the study of Science. Their lack of familiarity with health matters and the belief of many that all illness is amenable to Scientific healing suggests that they place little emphasis on early detection. Even if they are disposed to seek medical diagnosis or treatment in some cases, they may not recognize the severity of their symptoms or be aware of the availability of appropriate medical facilities.

Although Scientists sometimes sacrifice their lives on the altar of their faith either through a desire to rely on Science or because of their naïveté in health matters, some factors operate to protect their health. A consideration of these factors suggests a modification of our usual conceptions of health, illness, and sick-role behaviours. These are usually defined as behaviours intentionally aimed at preventing, detecting, and healing illness,[47] but it seems worthwhile to view behaviour in terms of its latent functions as well as its manifest functions.[48] In other words, health, illness, and sick-role behaviours may be either intentional or unintentional.

Some examples will indicate how Scientists unintentionally engage in these behaviours. An obvious first point is Scientists' relatively low use of alcohol and, especially, tobacco. Though these items appear not to have been proscribed primarily to protect health,[49] the latent function is a low incidence of lung cancer[50] and probably emphysema, chronic bronchitis, coronary problems, cirrhosis of the liver, etc.

Further, visits to health personnel for 'legitimate' reasons may result in the detection and consequent treatment of other ailments. Routine prophylactic dental visits provide one example; [51] existing cavities may be detected and filled, other cavities may be prevented, and oral pathology of other types may be discovered at an early stage. Beauty is sought but both beauty and health are obtained. Another example is provided by visits to physicians for the alleviation of pain, a practice legitimated by Mrs Eddy. [52] If the pain is determined to be symptomatic of a mechanical problem, the patient generally will accept medical treatment. Even if the problem is not a mechanical one, the patient probably stands a fair chance of receiving medical treatment, for physicians appear generally to attempt tactfully to convince their Scientist patients that treatment is necessary and sensible. [53]

Finally, although in some cases family members and friends encourage those who are apparently troubled with a physical problem to rely entirely on Scientific treatment, in other cases they request, cajole, or compel Scientists to protect their health and submit to medical treatment. Family members are probably most effective in this respect. If the students in the sample give an accurate indication of the degree of religious heterogeneity in the families of Scientists generally, many marriages are exogamous. Only 65 per cent of the students reported that both their parents embraced Science, and in a number of these families only one spouse actively practised the religion or even belonged to The Mother Church, membership in which is basic to the practice of Science. To cite but one instance of parental influence, a student had a physician remove a cinder from her eye because her non-Scientist father urged her to do so. He told her that he had confidence in her ability ultimately to handle the matter Scientifically, but that she might have to put up with considerable unnecessary discomfort until she achieved an understanding of the illusory nature of her affliction; a physician, on the other hand, would be able rapidly to remedy her problem, thus giving her more time to concentrate fully on her study of Science. Other students described pressures exerted by non-Scientist friends and room-mates. Since 62 per cent of them reported that none of their five best friends was a Scientist,[54] such pressures apparently are not uncommon. Scientists may, then, engage in actions that protect their health in order not to disrupt satisfying relationships with other people.

Behaviour and Beliefs of the Larger Society

A number of commonly-held beliefs and consequent actions of non-Scientists enhance the viability of Christian Science. First, supernatural beliefs are quite prevalent in modern societies. The Scientific belief system is unique, but many individuals have strong beliefs in faith healing and some large denominations as well as small sects and cults have institutionalized faith healing; witness the Roman Catholic shrine at Lourdes and healing movements within various Protestant churches. Even many persons who do not themselves rely on faith healing believe that it is often effective, for spiritual healing has had a place in Christianity since its inception. Although many people think that Christian Scientists go too far in their reliance on what the majority of the population mistakenly regard as faith healing,[55] their own beliefs in similar supernatural phenomena, coupled with a strong tradition of religious freedom, result in few attempts to prevent Scientists from practising their religion or to convince them that spiritual treatment alone is unnecessary and unsafe.

Second, many health-related beliefs are cultural truisms in industrialized societies. For example, virtually everybody believes that aspirin is an effective remedy for most headaches and that poliomyelitis can be prevented by immunization. Since these beliefs are seldom challenged, there is no need to devote valuable television and classroom time to their espousal. Nor is it necessary to rebut the doctrine of 'animal magnetism',[56] for very few persons believe in and fear it. Of course, it is impossible for a Scientist entirely to avoid exposure to un-Scientific information, such as TV commercials for patent medicines, health campaigns, etc., but little information that directly contradicts Scientific beliefs is cogently presented to Scientists.

Third, public officials or functionaries of organizations may exert either legal or extralegal power to compel Scientists to protect their health and the health of their families. For example, physical examinations for military service, participation in organized athletics, attendance at schools, and some types of employment are often required for Scientists and non-Scientists alike. Courts sometimes order parents and guardians to provide medical care for their dependents,[57] and even adult Scientists are sometimes forcibly taken to physicians and hospitals.[68] (One student, for example, was delivered to a hospital after a motor accident even though she asked the police only to take her home.) Since the success of medical treatment is often ascribed to concurrently-utilized Christian Science, even involuntary medical care can serve to strengthen Scientists' faith in the efficacy of their religion.

Various characteristics of individuals, Christian Science, and secular society minimize the disconfirming impact of reality on Scientific beliefs, but it is doubtful that Science could survive were it not for one final set of factors. The good health enjoyed by most Christian Scientists in America, Britain, and other developed nations appears to be due primarily to the health status of the general populace and the actions taken by individuals and public agencies to safeguard that health. Christian Scientists may not concern themselves with the purity of the water they drink, but others do. Non-Scientists have eradicated the breeding grounds of anopheline mosquitoes, fought a continuing battle against venereal diseases, and all but eradicated smallpox, typhus, and typhoid. The religion may survive, therefore, because it is not very harmful to the health of Scientists.

A Note on the Current Status and Prospects of Christian Science

These, then, are hypothesized reasons for the continuing existence of Christian Science. A balanced perspective also requires consideration of evidence that suggests its stagnation or decline. Wilson points out that data on the number of Christian Science churches, societies,[59] and practitioners indicate that the sect may at present be experiencing a decline in Britain, the United States, and some other areas,[60] and Kinsolving concurs.[61] Further, Wilson contends that 'as far as numbers of churches go, Christian Scientists in recent years have grown in numbers only in certain states, particularly in those to which older people retire'[62]; and Kinsolving says that of thirty-five persons attending a recent Sunday service in a Massachusetts church (which could hold at least 350 persons), 'there were only three people who looked younger than 60 or 70: the virile and hirsute young soloist and two admiring young females'.[63] It is likely that many – perhaps most – adult Scientists are converts, many of whom turned to Christian Science for solutions to problems for which medical science had been of little or no help.[64] Many young Scientists, especially those who are well-educated, find it difficult entirely to accept Christian Scientific conceptions of etiology and to rely totally on Scientific treatment.[65]

Some scholars believe that religion in general is declining in popularity, although others speak of a religious revival.[66] Since Christian Science Church policy (and it is not unique in this respect) proscribes publication of membership figures, it is difficult to determine precisely whether or not Christian Science is declining (if it is declining) more rapidly than many other religions, but it is probably the case that Christian Science has passed its prime.

Christian Science was founded by an American and Scientists do not engage in formal missionary work, which factors undoubtedly affect the spatial distribution of adherents. But perhaps it is not coincidental that Christian Science has few followers in under-developed parts of the world, where morbidity and mortality rates are high. In all of Africa, only thirty-seven churches and societies exist, and thirty-one of these are in the European citadels of Rhodesia and the Republic of South Africa. In Asia there are only twenty organized groups, and Central America (including Mexico and excluding the Canal Zone) and South America have, respectively, three and twenty-six organizations. In the United States, however, there are about 2,400 groups, and approximately 290 may be found in Great Britain and another 113 in West Germany.[67] In other words, Christian Science may flourish only where it is least detrimental to the health of its adherents.

NOTES AND REFERENCES

1 Suggestion, sometimes referred to as 'animal magnetism', is of various types, including at least the following: drug advertisements and other references to illness in the mass media of communication; utterances of individuals; unvoiced thoughts, either benign or malevolent, of individuals; and autonomous, vitalistic thought. These topics are dealt with in detail in Arthur E. Nudelman, 'Christian Science conceptions of treatment and etiology of illness: An empirical study', Dept. of Sociology, Old Dominion University, Virginia, mimeo., 1974; A. M. Bellwald, *Christian Science and the Catholic Faith,* Macmillan, New York, 1922; Charles S. Braden, *Christian Science Today,* Southern Methodist University Press, Dallas, Texas, 1958; Christian Science Publishing Society (ed.), *What is Animal Magnetism?,* Christian Science Publishing Society, Boston, Mass., 1969; Georgine Milmine, *The Life of Mary Baker G. Eddy and the History of Christian Science,* Doubleday, New York, 1909.

2 *Science and Health with Key to the Scriptures,* Trustees under the Will of Mary Baker G. Eddy, Boston, Mass., 1906, p. 472.

3 See, for example, Leon Festinger, Henry W. Riecken, and Stanley Schachter, *When Prophesy Fails,* University of Minnesota Press, Minneapolis, Minn., 1956; Jane A. Hardyck and Marcia Braden, 'Prophesy fails again,' *Journal of Abnormal and Social Psychology,* Vol. 65, August 1962, pp. 136-141; John Lofland, *Doomsday Cult,* Prentice-Hall, Englewood Cliffs, New Jersey, 1966; J. L. Simmons, 'On maintaining deviant belief systems', *Social Problems,* Vol. 11, Winter 1964, pp. 250-256.

4 Of special relevance to this report are: Mary Baker Eddy, op. cit.; Idem, *Manual of the Mother Church: The First Church of Christ, Scientist* (89th ed.), Trustees under the Will of Mary Baker G. Eddy, Boston, Mass., 1908; Christian Science Publishing Society (ed.), op. cit.

5 Braden, op. cit.; R. W. England, 'Some aspects of Christian Science as reflected in letters of testimony', *American Journal of Sociology,* Vol. 59, March 1954, pp. 448-453; Henry H. Goddard, 'The effects of mind on body as evidenced by faith cures', *American Journal of Psychology,* Vol. 10, April 1899, pp. 431-502; Joseph K. Johnson, *A Case Study of a Religion as a Form of Adjustment Behaviour,* unpublished Ph.D. dissertation, Dept. of Sociology, Washington University, 1937; Idem, 'Institutional adaptations of an urban religious movement', *Southwestern Social Science Quarterly,* Vol. 18, December 1937, pp. 255-261; Harold W. Pfautz, 'Christian Science: a case study of the social psychological aspect of secularization', *Social Forces,* Vol. 34, March 1956, pp. 246-251; Walter I. Wardwell, 'Christian Science healing', *Journal for the Scientific Study of Religion,* Vol. 4, April 1965, pp. 175-181; Idem, 'Christian Science and spiritual healing', in Richard H. Cox (ed.), *Religious Systems and Psychotherapy,* Charles C. Thomas, Springfield, Ill., 1973, pp. 72-88; Bryan R. Wilson, 'The origins of Christian Science', *Hibbert Journal,* Vol. 57, January 1959, pp. 161-170; Idem, *Sects and Society,* University of California Press, Berkeley, Calif., 1961; Idem, *Religious Sects,* McGraw-Hill, New York, 1970.

6   Arthur E. Nudelman, 'Dimensions of religiosity: a factor-analytic view of Protestants, Catholics, and Christian Scientists', *Review of Religious Research,* Vol. 13, Fall 1971, pp. 42-56.

7   Idem, 'Christian Science and secular science: adaptation on the college scene', *Journal for the Scientific Study of Religion,* Vol. 11, September 1972, pp. 271-276.

8   Idem, 'Christian Science conceptions . . .'.

9   Arthur E. Nudelman and Barbara E. Nudelman, 'Health and illness behaviour of Christian Scientists', *Social Science and Medicine,* Vol. 6, April 1972, pp. 253-262.

10   David Mechanic, *Medical Sociology,* Free Press, New York, 1968, pp. 310-322.

11   Nudelman and Nudelman, op. cit.

12   Jerome D. Frank, *Persuasion and Healing* (rev. ed.), Johns Hopkins University Press, Baltimore, Maryland, 1973, pp. 73-74.

13   The students queried generally held one or both of the following conceptions of how practitioners assist in healing: (1) they counsel patients; (2) they 'work' for patients. 'Metaphysical work' was a hazy and undifferentiated phenomenon to the students (Nudelman, 'Christian Science conceptions . . .', op. cit.).

14   Joseph Jaffe and Walter H. Slote, 'Interpersonal factors in denial of illness', *Archives of Neurology and Psychiatry,* Vol. 80, November 1958, pp. 653-656.

15   *Science and Health . . .* , p. 161.

16   Jack E. Biersdorf and John R. Johnson, Jr., 'Religion and physical disability', *Rehabilitation Record,* Vol. 7, January-February 1966, pp. 1-4.

17   Braden, op. cit., p. 7.

18   According to Wardwell ('Christian Science and spiritual healing', p. 75), 'the vast proportion of Christian Science cures ("demonstrations") of physical complaints ("claims") involve vague aches and pains, often internal or afflicting muscles, bones, or joints (e.g., arthritis). Improved mobility is a major manifestation in Christian Science cures. Many such physical disabilities are presumably partly psychogenic or psychosomatic in origin. Since critics have frequently alleged that Christian Science cures by suggestion, it could be a source of embarrassment to call attention to the benefits that Christian Science provides to the psychologically ill.'

19   *Science and Health . . .* , pp. 401-402.

20   Ibid., p. 329.

21   Ibid., p. 388.

22   'Claims' are 'claims of matter'; they include, in addition to physical and mental illness, interpersonal difficulties, academic or occupational problems, unhappiness, poverty, lost articles, and other problems.

23   When asked whether or not friends and family would expect less from them when they are sick, 90 per cent of the students in the sample stated

that they would be excused from their normal role obligations. One student who gave a negative response admitted that her mother would serve her meals in bed when she was not feeling well.

When utilizing Science, one must deny that one has a problem and affirm the Truth of one's perfection, for to recognize the existence of a problem militates against Scientific healing. This would appear to present Scientists with a dilemma: by doing 'metaphysical work' to heal an ailment and by seeking release from role obligations that they cannot perform, are they not *ipso facto* admitting that they have a problem? Few students in the sample appeared to recognize the dilemma, but it is noted in official Christian Science literature, for example, Roy G. Watson, 'The Church's broad responsibility in handling animal magnetism', in Christian Science Publishing Society (ed.), *What is Animal Magnetism?* op. cit., pp. 27-35.

24　*Science and Health . . .* , p. 147.

25　*Manual . . .* , article **XXXV**, section 1.

26　*Science and Health* had gone through 382 editions by 1906. The edition number was omitted from the copyright page after 1906, but it is probable that Mrs Eddy made more changes prior to her death in 1910 (Braden, op. cit., p. 278). According to the *Manual,* the current version of this work is the 89th edition.

27　Braden, op. cit., pp. 279-281.

28　Ibid., p. 285.

29　Article VIII, section 16.

30　Eddy, *Science and Health . . .* , pp. 61-62.

31　'Checking overpopulation', *Christian Science Monitor,* 8 April, 1967, p.18.

32　Some students in the sample criticized Science for being too idealistic and Scientists for refusing to descend to a lower plane to converse and empathize with less successful members of the faith. One student, for example, thought that abstention from alcohol and tobacco should not be a requirement for membership in The Mother Church, but that one should be permitted to join before one achieves perfection and thus gain help in solving one's problems. Another student condemned as totally unrealistic the refusal of a practitioner to write to the appropriate U.S. Army official and suggest release of the student's boyfriend from active duty so that he could support his recently widowed and destitute mother. (The practitioner said that God would provide for the mother.)

33　*Science and Health . . .* , p. 179.

34　Nudelman, 'Christian Science and secular science . . .', op. cit.

35　Leon Festinger, *A Theory of Cognitive Dissonance,* Row, Peterson, Evanston, Ill., 1957; cf. William J. McGuire, 'Selective exposure: a summing up', in Robert P. Abelson *et al* (eds.), *Theories of Cognitive Consistency: A Sourcebook,* Rand McNally, Chicago, Ill., 1968, pp. 797-800.

36　A Christian Scientist high school language teacher whom I know does not sterilize the headphones in her language laboratory, although this is commonly recognized as essential to prevent transmission of ear infections among students. She doubts that her practice can harm the students and believes that to clean the headphones would be to admit the etiological significance of micro-organisms, which would, in Scientific belief, render her and her students susceptible to the illusion of disease.

37   Gale E. Wilson, 'Christian Science and longevity', *Journal of Forensic Sciences,* Vol. 1, October 1956, pp. 43-60.

38   *Science and Health* . . . , op. cit., p. 127.

39   Nudelman, 'Christian Science and secular science . . .', op. cit.

40   Leon Festinger, 'A theory of social comparison processes', *Human Relations,* Vol. 7, May 1954, pp. 117-140.

41   When asked whether or not it is difficult to be both a 'good' Christian Scientist and a college student, 35 per cent of the students acknowledged that they had, at one time or another, experienced doubts about their religion as a direct result of their academic work, and a few students had doubts about whether or not their academic majors were compatible with their faith. An engineering major, for example, thought that 'a really devout Christian Scientist wouldn't try to get involved in any material science.'

42   *Science and Health* . . . , op. cit., p. 345.

43   Ibid., p. 149.

44   Nudelman, 'Christian Science conceptions . . .', op. cit.

45   J. L. Simmons, op. cit., p. 253.

46   Godfrey M. Hochbaum, 'Why people seek diagnostic X-rays', *Public Health Reports,* Vol. 71, April 1956, pp. 377-380; Idem, *Public Participation in Medical Screening Programs,* Public Health Service Publication No. 572, U.S. Public Health Service, Washington, D.C., 1958; Irwin M. Rosenstock, Mayhew Derryberry, and Barbara K. Carriger, 'Why people fail to seek poliomyelitis vaccination', *Public Health Reports,* Vol. 74, February 1959, pp. 98-103; Irwin M. Rosenstock, 'What research in motivation suggests for public health', *American Journal of Public Health,* Vol. 50, March 1960, pp. 295-302; Idem, 'Prevention of illness and maintenance of health', in John Kosa, Aaron Antonovsky, and Irving K. Zola (eds.), *Poverty and Health,* Harvard University Press, Cambridge, Mass., 1969, pp. 168-190.

47   Stanislav V. Kasl and Sidney Cobb, 'Health behavior, illness behavior, and sick-role behavior', *Archives of Environmental Health,* Vol. 12, February 1966, pp. 246-266; April 1966, pp. 531-541.

48   Robert K. Merton, *Social Theory and Social Structure* (rev. ed.), Free Press, Glencoe, Ill., 1957, pp. 19-84.

49   De Witt, John, *The Christian Science Way of Life,* Prentice-Hall, Englewood Cliffs, New Jersey, 1962, p. 207.

50   G. E. Wilson, op. cit.

51   Seventy-five per cent of the students customarily received dental checkups and prophylactic treatment at least once a year. Only 6 per cent, all of whom had received dental care in the past on an irregular basis, said they

planned to do without dental care in the future.

52   *Science and Health* . . . , op. cit., p. 464.

53   Conversations with a few primary-care physicians suggest that tactful persuasion is sometimes at least partially successful in eliciting permission to proceed with treatment.

54   Nineteen per cent listed one Scientist among their five best friends, 12 per cent listed two, 4 per cent listed three, and 2 per cent listed four. (Rounding errors prevent the total from equalling 100 per cent.)

55   In a questionnaire study of 56 non-Scientists at the university from which the sample of Scientists was drawn, no respondent gave a response that could unequivocally be interpreted as indicating a basic familiarity with the sect. Most students simply stated that Scientists do not believe in medicine. When Scientific healing was mentioned, virtually all students referred to faith healing and God's miracles rather than to the understanding of Truth.

56   See note 1.

57   I. H. Rubenstein, 'Custody of infant children in medical neglect cases', *Journal of the American Medical Women's Association,* Vol. 16, October 1961, pp. 771-774.

58   Conversations with hospital officials indicate that although they are generally powerless to prevent 'legal suicide' of lucid adult patients who refuse medical care, hospital personnel usually operate in terms of an 'implied consent' doctrine if patients are comatose or otherwise not in full control of their faculties. As one administrator remarked of his hospital's experience with non-lucid Christian Scientists, Jehovah's Witnesses, and others with unusual beliefs regarding illness and medical treatment, 'We treat – and damn the torpedoes!' Few lawsuits result from such treatment.

59   A Christian Science organization qualifies for *church* status only if it has at least sixteen members, including four members of The Mother Church and one practitioner. A *society* may be formed when these stipulations cannot be met.

60   Bryan Wilson, *Religious Sects,* op. cit., pp. 149-152.

61   Lester Kinsolving, 'Inside religion: Christian Science declines', *Virginian-Pilot* (Norfolk, Va.), 1 July, 1973, p. C3.

62   Bryan Wilson, *Religious Sects,* op. cit., p. 149.

63   Kinsolving, op. cit.

64   De Witt, John, op. cit., p. 12.

65   Nudelman, 'Christian Science conceptions . . .', op. cit.; Idem, 'Christian Science and secular science . . .', op. cit.; Nudelman and Nudelman, op. cit.

66   N. J. Demerath III and Phillip E. Hammond, *Religion in Social Context,* Random House, New York, 1969, p. 193; Dean M. Kelley, *Why Conservative Churches are Growing,* Harper & Row, New York, 1972; Rodney Stark and Charles Y. Glock, *American Piety: The Nature of Religious Commitment,* University of California Press, Berkeley, Calif., 1968, pp. 204-224.

67   Christian Science Publishing Society, 'Churches of Christ, Scientist and Christian Science Societies', *The Christian Science Journal,* Vol. 93, February 1975, pp. 3-39.

Walter I. Wardwell

4

Orthodox and Unorthodox Practitioners: Changing Relationships and the Future Status of Chiropractors

I shall present a schematic outline of a way of conceptualizing changing relationships, and the potential for future changes in relationships, between orthodox physicians and various types of irregular, unorthodox, sectarian, and cult practitioners. My reference is to contemporary American society and similar cultures. Although I shall discuss systems of ideas, theories, and philosophies of healing, my major emphasis is on the actual social roles and relationships of the various groups and their institutional supports within the changing structure of society. For example, in the United States of America the roles and relationships of orthodox practitioners are supported by the American Medical Association along with colleges of medicine, the private foundations devoted to medical research, the pharmaceutical industry, the United States Public Health Service, and the examining and licensing boards of the fifty states, etc.

Irregular and unorthodox practitioners have also achieved varying degrees of legal recognition, popular acceptance, and toleration by organized medicine. They have their own professional associations, institutions for education and training, practice establishments such as offices and clinics, and suppliers of therapeutic devices and literature. I intend to include the entire range of irregular and cultist practitioners – from shamans and faith healers at one extreme to those accepted as only mildly unorthodox at the other, such as osteopaths, whose professional acceptance is currently far greater in the United States than in Great Britain and Canada.

Different dimensions of deviation by irregular and cultist practitioners from medical orthodoxy can be distinguished. One involves the role played by religious faith, magic, or supernatural entities in therapy. This dimension is represented by shamans, faith healers, and Christian Science practitioners. A second dimension concerns a related but secularized emphasis on the psychic side of the psychosomatic equation. Examples are hypnotists, Reichians, dianetics, and the 'group grope' therapies, represented by Esalen.[1] A third dimension involves alternative scientific theories or philosophies of what causes illness and of what therefore is appropriate therapy. The most prominent examples have been osteopathy, naturopathy, and chiropractic. These dimensions are not mutually exclusive and there is often overlap between them. Furthermore, there is psychosomatic involvement in all illness, mental or physical. The subdivision of orthodox practitioners into psychiatrists, on the one hand, and all other physicians, on the other, tends to conceal the interdependence of psychic and somatic elements in concrete illness.

I therefore prefer an alternative classification of non-orthodox practitioners based on such structural characteristics as legal licensure or customary practice. Using as a touchstone the medical profession, with its broad scope of practice, rights, and privileges, I have distinguished the following types of non-orthodox practitioners:[2]

1   *Ancillary practitioners*: those who practise directly under the supervision of orthodox physicians as assistants or technicians in diagnosis or therapy, e.g. nurses, physical therapists, inhalation therapists, hospital pharmacists, hospital audiologists, orthotists, prosthetists, etc. These groups achieve a stable subordinate-superordinate relationship with medicine that is threatened only when they seek greater professional autonomy or a broader scope of practice, as nurses and some physical therapists have recently been doing.

2   *Limited medical practitioners*: those who practise independent of medical supervision or direction but who limit their practices to specific conditions and/or parts of the human body, e.g. dentists,

podiatrists, optometrists, clinical psychologists, speech therapists, etc. Since these practitioners not only limit their scope of practice but also usually accept, at least implicitly, the authority of orthodox physicians over more serious or systemic illnesses, relations between these groups and orthodox medicine tend towards a stable, if sometimes somewhat symbiotic, *modus vivendi.*

3   *Marginal, or parallel, practitioners*: those who treat a wide range of human diseases but whose philosophy or theory of health and disease conflicts with that of orthodox medicine. Theoretical differences usually centre on the extent of the body's inherent curative powers, and on techniques for aiding, stimulating, or releasing them. Chiropractors have been the most prominent recent example although their differences with orthodox medicine appear to be attenuating; historically osteopaths also fitted into this category, though that is far less true in the United States today; still another example are naturopaths, a small group now tending to merge with chiropractors. Because these professions challenge some of the basic assumptions of orthodox medicine and attract patients with a wide variety of conditions, they pose a more serious threat to organized medicine. Relations between it and them are fraught with conflict and are inherently unstable.

4   *Quasi-practitioners*: those who reject the medical model of the doctor-patient relationship yet assist people in obtaining relief, e.g. faith healers, Christian Science practitioners, shamans, folk healers, and even well-intentioned quacks. If their rationale is religious or magical, these practitioners do not compete with orthodox physicians on the same ground; thus physicians can sometimes collaborate with them precisely for that reason. If such practitioners resort to devices of dubious scientific value (e.g. orgone boxes, or machines that emit radiations or other electrical impulses), to esoteric foods (e.g. 'royal jelly'), or to such practices as rejuvenating inoculations, their threat to orthodox medicine is usually so narrowly based as to constitute little challenge to it. Since organized medicine can 'fight quackery' or tolerate faith healing without any real threat to its epistemological underpinnings or to the incomes of its practitioners, it can do so pretty much altruistically and in the

name of the health of the general public. (When, on the other hand, it attempts to dismiss parallel professions like osteopathy or chiropractic as quackery, it runs the risk of being accused of a conflict of interest or of ulterior motives, and it is in fact usually so accused.)

These distinctions and categories of practitioners illustrate the range of possibilities for innovation, evolution, and change within and between the various healing cults, especially in so far as they provide models of alternative relationships to orthodox medicine. What factors *push* or *inhibit* evolution of a group of irregular practitioners towards a different type, or towards medical orthodoxy? The principal one is the stance that orthodox medicine itself takes towards the healing cult, which mainly depends on how much threat it senses from the unorthodox group. As noted above, the most serious challenge comes from marginal, or parallel, professions rather than from limited medical practitioners, with whom organized medicine can usually reach an accommodation. Since for marginal or parallel practitioners neither accommodation nor vigorous opposition is a wholly satisfactory ultimate goal or day-to-day strategy, the choice by organized medicine is likely to be a defensive tactic of containment. Its stance towards a particular irregular group will also vary depending on such other considerations as: (a) the number of marginal healing groups in existence at a given time; (b) the relative size, popular support, and political influence of each; (c) the degree of solidarity or fragmentation within the unorthodox practitioner group; (d) the effectiveness of the group's leadership; and (e) whether the unorthodox group is seeking to maintain independence and distance from orthodox medicine or striving for some kind of acceptance, toleration, or even incorporation within medicine.

Furthermore, the extent to which accommodation between an irregular group and orthodox medicine is possible very much depends on: (a) how compatible or incompatible the epistemological, philosophical, or scientific bases of the group are with those of orthodox medicine; (b) how compatible the therapeutic techniques or modalities of the group are with those of orthodox medicine; (c) how high are the educational, professional, and ethical standards of the group; (d) how willing the unorthodox practitioners are to subordinate themselves to medical supervision or prescription (like ancillary practitioners) or alternatively to limit the scope of their practice or therapeutic techniques (like limited practitioners), for in neither of these two cases would they challenge the right of orthodox physicians to define what illness is and what the major parameters of diagnosis and treatment are: and (e) how acceptable the irregular group would be as regular professional colleagues.

As an example, consider the merger in 1961 of the California Osteopathic Association with the California Medical Society and the conversion of California College of Osteopathic Physicians and Surgeons to a medical school. The impetus for these changes came partly from the desire of the medical profession to incorporate osteopathy and partly from those osteopaths who wanted to become fully-fledged medical practitioners and felt no incompatibility between the way they and allopathic physicians conceptualize health, disease and therapy. Of course the California physicians also had to be willing to accept osteopaths as professional colleagues.[3] By contrast the Christian Science definition of illness as illusion and error and its prayerful technique of healing through reading from Mary Baker Eddy's *Science and Health with Key to the Scriptures* renders dialogue between its practitioners and physicians nearly impossible, despite the fact that a few medical doctors have converted to Christian Science throughout the past century. However, there have been a few cases of successful cooperation by orthodox physicians with folk healers and shamans, especially where non-Western peoples retain faith in native healers and where the disability is neurotic or psychogenic in origin. Pattison, a western-trained psychiatrist, cites an impressive cure of a disturbed Yakima Indian girl in central Washington whose possession by ghosts was exorcized by native practitioners at his suggestion.[4]

The strength of opposition to orthodox medicine by the irregular group also depends on how solidary or schismatic it is and on the orientations of its (often charismatic) leaders. Precisely because being unorthodox implies variation along one of the dimensions of deviance referred to earlier, leaders often differ as to how far along that dimension it is proper to be. Usually the original position is one of maximum deviation from orthodoxy, which may be followed by a ('backsliding') movement attenuating the difference. The split between chiropractic 'straights' and 'mixers' is a prototypical example. B. J. Palmer, son of the 'Founder of Chiropractic', himself known as the 'Developer of Chiropractic', was an extremely charismatic leader who urged his 'straight' followers to adhere to 'pure and unadulterated chiropractic'. He specifically meant by this no admixture of 'medical' or 'naturopathic' practices such as dietary regulation, vitamin prescription, or use of physical therapy modalities. Having developed a large educational institution and a following to whom he sold a wide range of literature and adjuncts to practice, Palmer had a strong vested interest in maintaining chiropractic as 'separate and distinct' from medicine. His new terminology, according to which chiropractors *analyse* rather than *diagnose* cases, *adjust* patients rather than *treat* them, eliminate the *cause* of disease (i.e. 'subluxations') rather than *symptoms,* permitted him and his lawyers to argue that chiropractic is so different from medicine that it should be regulated by a separate set of laws, examining boards, and licensing procedures. The supportive institutions of separate chiropractic colleges, licensing laws, and examining boards have become so firmly established that it would be difficult for a merger between chiropractic and medicine to take place even if 'mixer' chiropractors were to desire it and if chiropractic's scientific differences from medicine were to disappear. A recent conference on 'The Research Status of Spinal Manipulative Therapy', conducted under Congressional mandate by the National Institute of Neurological Diseases and Stroke, established that there does indeed exist a common scientific basis for medical, osteopathic, and chiropractic manipulative therapy.[5] But much more than a shared scientific orientation will be required before these three professions grow into professional communion with each other.

Rapprochement is not aided by the fact that irregular practitioners are likely to be ambivalent over their unorthodoxy. Although they may envy the power, prestige, and security of regular physicians, they cannot reject their own distinctive basis for existence. Twenty years ago Peter New described the dilemma faced by osteopathic students uncertain whether they were becoming inferior physicians or uniquely qualified irregulars.[6] More recently David Sternberg has described the even more difficult plight of chiropractic students who realize that many people consider that the profession they are preparing to enter is stigmatized.[7] Yet both osteopaths and chiropractors have compensating advantages. Compared with most other occupations, any kind of doctor ranks high in the hierarchy of occupational prestige. Chiropractors surpass all the ancillary health professions in professional autonomy and income, and perhaps even such limited medical professions as optometry and podiatry. The fact that chiropractors are being appointed to regional health planning agencies throughout the United States testifies to their increasing acceptance as health professionals.

It is instructive to contrast chiropractors as marginal practitioners with Christian Science healers as quasi-practitioners. The histories of the two groups reveal many superficial resemblances. Both originated in the United States in the last third of the nineteenth century. Each was dominated for many years by a single charismatic leader who, though uneducated, became a prolific writer and established a publishing firm and marketed millions of tracts. Each jealously exercised personal control over the movement's development including its financial affairs. Each built a distinctive physical setting (the 'Fountainhead' of chiropractic at Davenport, Iowa; the 'Mother Church' in Boston, Massachusetts) that remains to this day the symbolic centre of the movement. Each waged mortal combat with a 'devil' – MAM ('Malicious Animal Magnetism') in the case of Mary Baker Eddy, and the AMA (American Medical Association) in the case of B. J. Palmer.

But these resemblances are overshadowed by one fundamental difference. Since as a religion Christian Science denies the reality of matter, the body, sickness, and death, it simply fails to share any common ground with medicine. Metaphysically they are worlds apart. Chiropractic, on the other hand, differs from medicine in this respect only in placing greater emphasis on the *vix medicatrix naturae*, the innate intelligence of the body that makes cures possible. Although both Christian Scientists and chiropractors object to medication, they do so for different reasons and with different results. Christian Scientists consider spiritual healing and *materia medica* to be polar opposites, which is true. B. J. Palmer claimed that chiropractic is the exact antithesis of medicine, which it is not. Although chiropractic may not achieve its therapeutic successes for the reasons it gives (something that is also often true of medicine), it nevertheless shares with medicine the capability of being studied scientifically, i.e. being empirically validated or invalidated. Thus the potential exists for reconciling the differences between them using scientific research.

This leads to the key question, which is what kind of professional relationships could chiropractors or Christian Scientists conceivably ultimately develop with organized medicine? Is it possible, for example, that chiropractors could function as ancillary practitioners to physicians, or that they could become limited medical practitioners, or that they could even become fully-fledged physicians, like osteopaths (in the U.S.A.)? For Christian Scientists these possibilities simply do not exist. Their rejection of material reality and of medical therapy is in principle final and complete, despite the fact that individual Christian Scientists, including Mary Baker Eddy herself, have on occasion resorted to medical treatment. Hence Christian Science could never merge into the medical mainstream. The most that a *religious* sect can evolve into is a *denomination* or *church*. A *healing* sect, such as homeopathy, osteopathy, or chiropractic has at least the theoretic capability of evolving into medical orthodoxy, which is what happened to homeopathy around the turn of the century and is happening today to osteopathy.

Are there any chances of it happening to chiropractic? The 'official' pronouncements of the American Medical Association that chiropractic is 'quackery', that chiropractors even if sincere are bumbling incompetents, and that there is not a scintilla of evidence for chiropractic theory, would lead most people to a negative conclusion.[8] But consider the following evidence that chiropractors have already achieved a professional standing not very far below that of orthodox physicians: (1) In 1974 the last state to do so (Louisiana) licensed chiropractors. (2) In 1974 the United States Office of Education authorized an organization known as the Commission on Chiropractic Education to be the official accrediting agency for chiropractic colleges. (3) All chiropractic colleges now require applicants to have a minimum of two years of pre-professional college credits. (4) The laws of thirty-eight states now require candidates for a licence to practice chiropractic to have completed two years of pre-professional college work followed by a standard four-year course in a chiropractic college, while fifteen states require that chiropractic candidates pass the same examinations in basic science subjects that medical and osteopathic candidates take. (5) Medical schools now regularly invite chiropractors to lecture to their students on what chiropractic is and how chiropractors practise. (6) In 1972 Congress made chiropractors eligible to receive Medicare payments for professional services. (7) Most insurance companies now include payment for chiropractic services in their policies. (8) In Ontario, where there is a form of socialized medicine, chiropractors are recompensed just as medical doctors are from general tax funds; thus chiropractic treatments are available as a matter of right to all Ontario citizens who desire them.

These advances in education, popular acceptance, legal standing, and remuneration of chiropractors put great pressure on organized medicine to revaluate its stance towards them in the legal and political arenas as well as at the level of interprofessional exchange. Physician referrals of patients *to* chiropractors as well as acceptance of patients *from* chiropractors are increasing, together with the performance of customary professional courtesies. An external source of pressure towards accommodation between chiropractors and organized medicine comes from the movement towards a national health care system in the United States, which will require resolution of the question of how chiropractors and other marginal professions fit in. The answer has already been found for osteopaths: they will be treated like orthodox physicians. Naturopaths will probably be treated similarly to chiropractors.

Certainly some solution to the state of unresolved tension between chiropractors and the system of orthodox medical care is needed.

What kind of relationship then is it most likely that chiropractors and orthodox physicians will eventually achieve? It is not at all probable that chiropractors, with their current legal, political, social and economic standing, will be content to accept the sub-ordinate status of practising under medical prescription, although that arrangement would be the most acceptable to organized medicine and would unambiguously legitimize chiropractors within the health care system. In view of the specialized nature of spinal manipulative therapy and the expertise required to determine when it is indicated, contraindicated, or should be modified during a course of treatment, a physician untrained in manipulative therapy would not know when to prescribe it or when not to. In fact, because of the many years of negative pronouncements from the AMA about spinal manipulative therapy, it would be unlikely that many physicians would prescribe spinal manipulative therapy at all!

On the other hand, it is equally unlikely that chiropractic will follow the path of osteopathy towards fusion with medicine. There are too many obstacles from both the medical and the chiropractic sides. Chiropractic is still very much limited in the range of its therapeutic techniques. Nowhere are chiropractors permitted to prescribe drugs or perform major surgery, nor have they been trained to do so. In only a handful of states can they practise obstetrics, perform minor surgery, or set simple fractures, and even in those states only a minority of chiropractors undertake those procedures. Furthermore, despite the wide range of illnesses and conditions that chiropractors have claimed to benefit, the vast bulk of chiropractic practice is concerned with musculo-skeletal problems. Most chiropractors are also still philosophically opposed to medication as a major thereapeutic strategy.

On the medical side the opposition to chiropractors remains intense, not only organizationally, but in the minds and attitudes of individual physicians. While some physicians are becoming curious or even convinced about the value of chiropractic treatment for a limited range of conditions, they are not yet ready to welcome chiropractors as fraternal colleagues in the general practice of medicine. Physicians are still suspicious of chiropractors' educational and professional qualifications and of the possibility that chiropractors may try to treat 'medical' conditions beyond their ability to help, or even to diagnose. Organizationally they would prefer that if spinal manipulation is to be incorporated within the medical armamentarium of therapeutic techniques at all it should be performed by physical therapists under physician prescription and supervision. Since the medical profession is still undergoing digestive cramps from its efforts to swallow up osteopathy, it is not yet ready to try to absorb chiropractic.

The most likely compromise is that chiropractors will evolve into something like limited medical practitioners, although it may take a long time. The pressures pushing chiropractors in this direction are fairly strong. In addition to their legal and philosophically-based restriction to spinal manipulative therapy some chiropractors choose to limit their practices to an especially narrow range of muscle and joint strains and sprains. Among the reasons why they do so are: (a) patients more readily associate chiropractors with these conditions; (b) there is an obvious and direct relationship between chiropractic therapy and such conditions; (c) physicians co-operate more readily with a chiropractor who defines his professional role in this way; (d) it is a 'safer' and more cautious mode of practice than to treat systemic conditions or those involving internal organs; and (e) realistically it is no doubt true that spinal manipulative therapy has limits to its benefits and is not a panacea for all illnesses. Not only do some state laws restrict chiropractors to adjustment of spinal segments by hands only, but Medicare and many insurance companies limit payment of chiropractors' fees to such treatments. Although chiropractors object strenuously to the narrowness of this interpretation of their role and function, its effect is to further limit their scope of practice and to push them in the direction of being limited practitioners.

With laws, repayment provisions, insurance companies, physicians, and patients all pressuring chiropractors to narrow the range of conditions they treat, and with patients, as well as other health professionals, generally unconvinced that chiropractors can provide complete health care, chiropractors may some day accept a redefinition of their professional role from 'marginal' to 'limited'. Despite the more modest nature of the therapeutic claims that could be made and the real restriction of their scope of practice that such a designation implies, it would confer some real advantages on chiropractors. It would give them a recognized position in the health care system, a fact of considerable importance inasmuch as a federally financed health care system is envisaged in the relatively near future. It would remove the stigma of 'cult', 'quackery', 'irregular', etc., now associated with chiropractic. It would eliminate some of the ambiguity concerning how chiropractors are expected to practise (although I would expect that some chiropractors would continue to treat a wide range of conditions which they believe chiropractic can benefit). Finally, the status of being a limited practitioner is quite a reasonable compromise between being an ancillary practitioner or a fully-qualified primary care provider when neither of these alternatives is a real possibility.

Of course the alternative is still possible that the status quo will be preserved and that chiropractors will remain a marginal profession. To argue that a limited medical status is a plausible compromise is not to guarantee that it will happen. What the analytic scheme that has been described does is to clarify the possibilities and to make easier the analysis of the factors pushing or inhibiting the evolution of any unorthodox health profession towards another or towards orthodoxy. Chiropractors have been treated as a prototypical example of an unorthodox health profession whose fate is illumined by this analytic scheme.

NOTES AND REFERENCES

1 Joseph Havens, 'Gestalt, bioenergetics, and encounter: new wine without wineskins', in Richard H. Cox (ed.), *Religious Systems and Psychotherapy*, Charles C. Thomas, Springfield, Illinois, 1973.

2 Walter I. Wardwell, 'Limited, marginal, and quasi-practitioners', in Howard E. Freeman, Sol Levine and Leo G. Reeder (eds.), *Handbook of Medical Sociology*, Prentice-Hall, Englewood Cliffs, New Jersey, 1972.

3   American Osteopathic Association, *White Paper: AOA-AMA Relation-ships, No. 2,* Chicago, Illinois, 1968. The fact that those osteopaths who were board-certified as specialists later failed to receive recognition by the corresponding medical boards is still a bone of contention between the two groups.

4   E. Mansell Pattison, 'Exorcism and psychotherapy: a case of collaboration', in Richard H. Cox (ed.), op. cit.

5   These papers will be published as a monograph in July 1975 in the series of the National Institute of Neurological Diseases and Stroke, US Public Health Service, Department of Health, Education and Welfare.

6   Peter New, 'The osteopathic students: a study in dilemma', in E. Gartly Jaco (ed.), *Patients, Physicians and Illness,* Free Press, Glencoe, Illinois, 1958.

7   David Sternberg, *Boys in Plight: A Case Study of Chiropractic Students Confronting a Medically-Oriented Society,* Ph.D. dissertation in Sociology, New York University, 1969. Available through Xerox University Micro-films, Ann Arbor, Michigan.

8   H. Thomas Ballantine (Chairman of the AMA Committee on Quackery), 'Will the delivery of health care be improved by the use of chiropractic services?' *New England Journal of Medicine,* Vol. 286, 3 February, 1972, pp. 237-242.

PART TWO:

BELIEFS, ORGANIZATION AND FOLLOWING
OF MARGINAL MEDICAL GROUPS

Roy Wallis

5

Dianetics: A Marginal Psychotherapy[1]

While the therapeutic practices of pre-literate peoples have received much close scholarly attention, those which fall outside the dominant medical-psychiatric orthodoxy of industrial societies have received consideration of a mainly superficial kind, directed to journalistic reportage or medical polemic. But for exemplary studies of chiropractors,[2] osteopaths,[3] and Christian Scientists,[4] social scientific examination of unorthodox therapeutic practice in advanced societies has been extremely limited.[5] In the belief that such studies are not only of intrinsic interest but provide an insight into the strains and tensions generated by industrial societies, and unorthodox modes of coping with them, an account is presented here of a marginal therapeutic system, Dianetics, which emerged briefly into prominence in the early 1950s.

Dianetics was the discovery of L. Ron Hubbard, an American of colourful biography who had been an explorer, aviator, sailor and pulp fiction writer. In 1948 and 1949, Hubbard began to formulate a theory of mental functioning and an associated therapeutic practice, with which he experimented on a small group of followers in New Jersey. Among these followers was a book publisher, and John W. Campbell, the editor of a science-fiction magazine. Campbell was a man of considerable influence on the magazine's substantial readership and after having a persistent sinusitis condition alleviated by Dianetics, he promoted it actively through the magazine, *Astounding Science Fiction.*[6]

Campbell's excitement with this new discovery was readily conveyed to his readers, and numerous enquiries began to descend

77

upon the magazine's editorial offices, asking for treatment by, or information on, the practice. In April 1950, Hubbard and his associates established the Hubbard Dianetic Research Foundation, and in the following weeks an article by Hubbard[7] and a book describing the theory and practice were published. The trickle of enquiries turned into a deluge and the book *Dianetics: The Modern Science of Mental Health*[8] rapidly became a bestseller.

Theory and Practice of Dianetics

Hubbard presented a model of the mind which divided it into two parts.[9] Its main component was the *analytical* mind which functioned with computer-like efficiency, as long as its operation was not impeded by the *reactive* mind. While the analytical mind was a thoroughly rational unit with capacities considerably greater than those exhibited by most human beings, the reactive mind was thoroughly irrational, and prevented the analytical mind from achieving its full potential. The reactive mind had evolved, Hubbard argued, as a means of protecting the delicate machinery of the analytical mind. In the face of pain, emotional trauma or other threat to the individual's survival, the analytical mind 'shut off' and the reactive mind, a more robust mechanism, came into operation. The reactive mind was a perfect recording device, storing 'perceptic' details of the entire period when the analytic mind was not operating, and directing the organism in ways which had, according to information stored in its 'memory bank', previously led to the organism's survival. Hence even during periods of what were normally construed as unconsciousness, the reactive mind would be recording. Such recordings, containing all the 'perceptic' details of periods of pain, unconsciousness, emotional loss or trauma, and containing all the associated affect, were known as *engrams.*

At some future date should the individual enter an environment which contained any of this perceptic content, the analytical mind would begin to shut off, the reactive mind would come into operation and the individual would experience some of the pain originally contained in the engram, as a warning to leave the situation of danger. If, in the formation of the engram, words were spoken, these words might have a later effect similar to that of a post-hypnotic suggestion. If the words were subsequently repeated, the engram would be 'keyed-in' or partially restimulated, and could subsequently lead the individual to behave in 'aberrated' ways, suffer physical or mental illness, or otherwise impair his capabilities.

One of Hubbard's more radical discoveries was that the most important engrams, in terms of their effects on later behaviour and performance, were formed during intra-uterine life. Many examples are given in his book *Dianetics: The Modern Science of Mental Health,* and most of these involve violence of some kind, either between the parents of the foetus, or directed at the foetus in the form of unsuccessful abortion attempts. One case that he reports involved eighty-one abortion attempts, which he does not hesitate to call 'an incredible number'.[10]

An example of such an engramic situation is described as follows:

> Fight between mother and father shortly after conception. Father strikes mother in stomach. She screams (first percepts are pain, pressure, sound of blow and scream) and he says, 'God damn you, I hate you! You are no good. I'm going to kill you!' Mother says, 'Please don't hit me again. Please don't. I'm hurt. I'm hurt. I'm frantic with pain!' Father says, 'Lie there and rot, damn you! Goodbye!'[11]

Hubbard observes that such an engram can produce disease ('and rot'), or lead the 'aberree' (i.e. the individual with the engram, in this case, the foetus in later life) to feel other people are no good ('You are no good'), and to feel hostility towards them ('I hate you'). A similar case is presented as follows:

> Now let us take an engram from a girl patient whose father was badly aberrated. He strikes mother because he is afraid mother is pregnant. . . . Father: 'Get out! Get out! I know you haven't

been true to me! You were no virgin when I married you. I should have killed you long ago! Now you're pregnant. Get out!'

The girl, some five weeks after conception, is knocked 'unconscious' by the blow to mother's abdomen. She has a severe engram here because it has painful emotional value which she will never be able to dramatise satisfactorily. The aberrative pattern here demonstrates itself in hysterics whenever a man accuses her of not being true. She was a virgin when she was married twenty-one years after this engram was received, but she was sure she was not. She has had a 'childhood delusion' that her father was likely to kill her. And she is always afraid of being pregnant because it says *now* she is pregnant. . . .[12]

The purpose of Dianetic therapy (known as auditing or processing) was to locate and gain access to engrams, and 'erase' them from the reactive mind, thus eradicating their effects in the form of psychosomatic illness, emotional tension, or lowered capability, by permitting the analytical mind to operate unimpeded. Exhausting the reactive mind of engrams would hence have a number of highly desirable consequences. The individual would become 'self-determined' rather than having his actions determined by his engrams. The analytical mind, being a perfect computer, would always supply the correct answer from the information fed in, when relieved of the engrams which lead to error.[13] The individual's IQ would rise dramatically. He would be free of all psychological or psychosomatic illness, his resistance to physical illness would be vastly improved, and he would be able to cure himself of other illnesses or injuries much more rapidly. His memory would vastly improve. He would, in short be a 'clear'.

The only obstacle to this desired state was that while 'locks' – severe restimulations of engrams – could be released by 'returning' the individual to the restimulating situation, releasing engrams and hence clearing the reactive mind required that the earliest engram (the 'basic-basic') be located and cleared. The therapy could then move on to later engrams.

Therapy proceeded in the following manner: The pre-clear (or patient) lay on a bed or couch in a quiet room, while the auditor (or therapist) sat beside him.

> The auditor tells him to look at the ceiling. The auditor says: 'When I count from one to seven your eyes will close.' The auditor counts from one to seven and keeps counting quietly and pleasantly until the patient closes his eyes. A tremble of the lashes will be noticed in optimum *reverie*.[14]

Hubbard insisted that this process of inducing 'Dianetic reverie' was quite different from hypnotism. To ensure against hypnotic suggestion, however, a 'canceller' was installed. That is, the pre-clear was told:

> 'In the future, when I utter the word *cancelled*, everything which I have said to you while you are in a therapy session will be cancelled and will have no force with you. Any suggestion I have made to you will be without force when I say the word *cancelled*. Do you understand?'[15]

The pre-clear was assured he would be aware of everything that happened. When the pre-clear had entered the state of reverie he was requested to return to childhood, to an incident involving a pleasant experience, and to go through it from the beginning, recounting all the perceptual detail that came up. This was to convey to the pre-clear the idea of what was expected of him. If he could not recall (or 'relive' in Hubbard's view) such an early incident, he was returned to a more recent incident.

After further preliminaries the auditor directed the pre-clear to return to 'basic-basic'. He did this by directing the 'file-clerk' (a hypothetical entity which 'monitored' the memory banks and selected appropriate material on request by the auditor) to return to the incident necessary to resolve the case. Generally, the basic-basic was not located so simply, however, and other engramic material would be brought up. This had to be 'reduced', that is the pre-clear was asked to return to the beginning of the incident and recount all the perceptual detail involved in the incident. He would be directed to recount this incident over and over again, until all the emotion involved in it was discharged.

The 'file-clerk' would then be asked for 'the next incident required to resolve this case', and the process would be repeated. Ideally, basic-basic would be located and erased and the pre-clear then progressively cleared of all subsequent engrams and locks. Often, however, this would not occur and it would therefore be necessary to end the session at some convenient point, usually after the 'reduction' of an engram or 'lock', i.e. when all the affect associated with a particular incident was discharged. A Dianetics session usually lasted around two hours, but might continue much longer if the pre-clear was 'stuck in an incident', i.e. an engram.

At the end of the session the pre-clear would be told to 'come up to present time'. The auditor might then question him as to the time, location, etc. to ensure that he was 'in present time'. He would then say 'cancelled' and end the session.

> . . . (work continues until the auditor has worked the patient enough for that period). . . . Come to present time. Are you in present time? (Yes) (Use canceller word). When I count from five to one and snap my fingers you will feel alert. Five, four, three, two, one. (snap).[16]

The thrust of the auditing activity was to get the pre-clear to return to the 'basic-area', i.e. the area of pre-natal experience; to contact the basic-basic engram and erase it; and then move along the 'time-track' erasing later-life engrams until the individual was cleared. In order to reach the basic-basic, however, it was often believed necessary first to reduce, or discharge, the painful emotion from later-life trauma which 'blocked' access to it. A variety of additional techniques existed to facilitate the pre-clear's return along the 'time-track'.

Hubbard viewed Dianetic therapy as a uniquely efficacious means of resolving psychosomatic illnesses (which he believed to include *at least* 70 per cent of all known illnesses).

Arthritis, dermatitis, allergies, asthma, some coronary difficulties, eye trouble, bursitis, ulcers, sinusitis, etc. form a very small section of the psychosomatic catalogue. Bizarre aches and pains in various portions of the body are generally psychosomatic. Migraine headaches are psychosomatic, and with the others, are uniformly cured by dianetic therapy. (And the word *cured* is used in its fullest sense.)[17]

Even the common cold was psychosomatic and those cleared by Dianetics did not suffer from colds,[18] and 'A number of germ diseases are predisposed and perpetuated by engrams. Tuberculosis is one.'[19] Hence, there were few ills to which mind or flesh are heir that could not be helped by Dianetics.

While Hubbard claimed only to be concerned with producing a theory of the mind and illness-formation on a functional basis, and argued that structural explanations for the phenomena generated by his practice, or for its success, would follow in years to come, he occasionally suggested structural hypotheses to guide further researchers:

> Arthritis of the knee, for instance, is the accumulation of all knee injuries in the past. The body confuses time and environment with the time and environment where the knee was actually injured and so keeps the pain there. The fluids of the body avoid the pain area. Hence a deposit which is called arthritis.[20]

Such matters, however, were of less concern to Hubbard than that of producing a theory and method which worked.

Dianetics was initially presented as a practice which anyone of normal intelligence could successfully undertake. A thorough knowledge of *Dianetics: The Modern Science of Mental Health* was thought to be all that was necessary, and hence interested persons could 'co-audit' each other on the basis of their knowledge of this work.[21] Professional courses were soon established, however, and those interested were encouraged to undertake four weeks' training at a fee of $500 to secure certification as a Hubbard Dianetic Auditor.

Membership and Motivations

While Hubbard's book drew many followers briefly to Dianetics, most abandoned it as rapidly as they had taken it up. A core of followers remained, however, and concerning these there is available a certain amount of demographic and motivational data.[22] The age distribution of Dianeticists peaked in the period 27-40 years of age, with the average age estimated to be about 38 years. The sex distribution showed a marked male over-representation, and the occupations of followers displayed a marked clustering in white-collar occupational categories. Manual workers were not typical and indeed the occupational data show a distinct tendency for members to have had professional, semi-professional, or other non-routine white-collar occupations. As one would therefore expect, the educational level of Dianeticists was higher than that for the general population. Most had completed secondary education and a large proportion had attended a college or university. Further available data show that Dianeticists were predominantly consumers of science fiction literature; they were largely protestants or agnostics; and many had already acquainted themselves with at least one quasi-philosophical-psychological system, such as Count Alfred Korzybski's General Semantics. They were also almost entirely white.

The divergence from the general pattern of followers of marginal therapeutic movements in western societies in which females are typically over-represented, is to be accounted for by the broader scope of Dianetics. Although heavily promoted as a therapeutic system, it did not restrict its domain to the area of physical healing. Rather, its therapeutic capacity was seen as particularly relevant to psychosomatic illness and psychological improvement. Thus much of its appeal was as a lay psychotherapy and self-improvement system rather than as merely a means of curing chronic physical illness. Motivations for taking up Dianetics can be seen as falling into three analytically distinct categories.

1 *The problem-solver*: Most individuals recruited to Dianetics were preoccupied with a concern for self-improvement based upon an acute awareness of their failure to attain the standards of

achievement in some area of life that were approved and reinforced in the society around them. Their concern might be for improvement of a physical, psychological or of a social kind. The search for therapeutic efficacy was a prominent source of motivation for many Dianeticists, who sought relief for themselves or other members of their families from conditions as diverse as cancer, schizophrenia, and agoraphobia. One published case history suggests such a motivation:

> DJ is a female, age 47, in the upper-middle income group, and married. In April, 1950, she began to be affected by severe pains in her right shoulder. The severity of the pain increased rapidly until she could barely move her right arm. A radiographic examination on June 8, 1950, showed a large calcareous deposit in the region of the subacromial bursa on the right side. Subsequent X-ray therapy, ending on July 9, 1950, failed to relieve her of any pain. When DJ arrived at the foundation on September 25, 1950, the pain of the bursitis was so severe that she could not move her right arm. Processing quickly uncovered the fact that her doctor had exclaimed during her birth, 'I think her shoulder is out of joint.'[23]

A large number of Dianeticists, although it is impossible to say what proportion they comprised, had a strong sense of capacities latent within them which could be brought to the surface if only a method could be found.

> It had always been for many, many years, a feeling of mine that one – specifically myself and by inference other human beings – don't [*sic*] perform with 100% efficiency, either mentally or physically, but mentally particularly. Hubbard's thesis . . . seemed to be a rational and satisfying explanation, and from that, the immediate urge was to try and do something about it.[24]

An English questionnaire respondent indicated that he had hoped Dianetics would prove the solution to his 'sense of frustration at not being able fully to use talents I possess'. Others admitted to a deep sense of inferiority or insecurity before they heard of Dianetics, which they hoped that it would enable them to overcome.

2 *The truth-seeker:* Many individuals were attracted to Dianetics when they came upon it at some point during a life-long search for meaning and truth. During the course of this search they had often examined the literature of popular philosophy and psychology, of religion, metaphysics and occultism. Science fiction, with its panoramic vision of man, time, and the cosmos, also provided many with an insight into the meaning of life and human behaviour. Dianetics, with its assertive claims to infallibility, offered to answer many of the questions which puzzled such individuals, and offered a practical and easily operationalized technique to put into effect the truths which it had uncovered. Others came into the orbit of Dianetics when some member of an amateur psychology or philosophy discussion group with which they were associated drew their attention to this development:

Well, we work away here on Dianetics. . . . Dianetics seems quite the best thing yet . . . although Jung's Analytical Psychology did give us more vivid inspiration.[25]

The original Houston Dianetics Society grew directly out of the local General Semantics Society. . . .[26]

3 *The career-oriented:* A small proportion of individuals were attracted to Dianetics as the source of an alternative career as a professional Dianeticist, or by the possibility that Dianetics was a revolutionary new therapeutic tool which would greatly improve their current practice as therapists. Dr Joseph Winter, the first Medical Director of the Hubbard Dianetic Research Foundation, exhibited this type of motivation. Winter was a doctor of medicine with little knowledge of psychiatry and psychology. He was unhappy with the trend in medicine towards greater specialization and compartmentalization, with the consequent absence of a vision of the patient as a whole. He had earlier sought this holism

in General Semantics, 'and while I agree with Korzybski that "the word is not the object", I found no satisfactory explanation for how such a confusion between levels of abstraction had arisen in the first place'.[27]

He sought answers to questions that medical science was unable to provide:

> I became aware again of the perplexity which plagues all doctors – the 'why' of human behaviour. I thought of all the questions which had gone unanswered or which had been answered in a tentative or equivocal manner – of questions which were frequently unasked because of their presumed unanswerability. Why did Mr M attempt to commit suicide? Why was it that Mrs E began to hear voices telling her to kill her newborn baby? Why did an intelligent man like Mr P find it necessary to drink a quart of whiskey every day? Why did Mrs T have coronary occlusion?
>
> The list of questions beginning with 'why' could be extended indefinitely. They all had one element in common: I knew of no satisfactory answer for any of them. The 'answers' and explanations which I had learned in medical school and which I passed on to my patients were superficial, taking into account only the preceding link in the chain of causality. A patient would ask me, 'Why does a person get coronary occlusion?' and I would answer glibly, 'Because there is a narrowing of the lumen of the coronary arteries.' And with that answer he would appear to be satisfied.[28]

Dr Winter, however, was not. He wanted to know why it had happened in this *particular* case, and how it could be treated or prevented. Dianetics, he and others similarly motivated believed, could prove the solution to these problems.

Social Organization and Development

With the publication of *Dianetics: The Modern Science of Mental Health* and the article in *Astounding,* Dianetics emerged organizationally in two forms. Organized around L. Ron Hubbard was the Hubbard Research Foundation, incorporated in April 1950 in Elizabeth, New Jersey. The Foundation had a Board of Directors, presided over by Hubbard. Branches were established in other major American cities, and by November 1950 there were branches in Los Angeles, New York, Washington, Chicago and Honolulu. The Foundations in Elizabeth and Los Angeles were offering an 'intensive, full-time course, lasting four weeks for professional auditors',[29] as well as courses of therapy, while the other Foundations mainly provided therapy.

The Board of Directors was composed of five others apart from Hubbard and his second wife Sara, including John W. Campbell, Joseph Winter, the publisher of *Dianetics: The Modern Science of Mental Health,* and C. Parker Morgan, a lawyer. Each Foundation had a staff of professional auditors and instructors, and those in New Jersey and Los Angeles briefly employed a small research staff of Dianeticists and trained psychologists. The Elizabeth Foundation had some thirty people on its staff. Numbers at the other Foundations fluctuated.

While an organizational structure was emerging within the Foundations, 'grass-roots' organizations of a rudimentary kind had emerged spontaneously. With the appearance of Hubbard's article and book, individuals all over America and in Great Britain began practising the technique. Many began with members of their own family or with friends, co-auditing each other, and enthusiastically proselytizing among their acquaintances. Some publicized their activities through advertisements in newspapers and magazines, or through newspaper stories. Some wrote to booksellers, or to the Foundations, to locate others in their area interested in the practice.

In this fashion, numerous small groups rapidly appeared with one or more enthusiasts organizing group activities, arranging meetings, and contacting members. These groups had a fluctuating membership, and little formal structure. They generally met one or two evenings a week. The 'senior' Dianeticist present (senior in the sense that he had been practising longest, or, less frequently, because he had taken some official training) would normally give a lecture, a demonstration, or conduct group-auditing. After a break, members would then team up in pairs for co-auditing.

Communication between the groups, between isolated individual followers, and between followers and the Foundations was initially largely by letter. The early followers were prolific correspondents. The more enthusiastic among them kept up correspondence with as many as a dozen others, detailing in their letters the cases they were 'running' (or auditing) at the time, the activities of their groups, new developments in theory and practice (whether retailed from official Dianetic sources or their own innovations), and rumours of administrative or political developments at the Foundations, as well as social and personal news. As some of these groups became established, however, mimeoed news-sheets were produced, along the lines of the 'fanzines' which link together science fiction enthusiasts. Cheaply produced, they provided a means for the leading independent figures and groups practising Dianetics to remain in contact with a dispersed and growing list of correspondents. These mimeoed bulletins were an important feature of Dianetics, providing the sense of a Dianetic community for the amateur following, as well as a later focus for, and a medium through which to express, discontent at the redirection of the movement by Hubbard.

The usual amateur bulletin would contain one or more articles on the theory or practice of Dianetics, discussions of cases audited, details of group meetings, information on innovations in theory and practice by recent graduates of Foundation courses or members of other groups, social information concerning figures in the Dianetic world, letters of encouragement or complaint, notices of recent publications, etc. The Foundation also issued a publication, in a slightly more sober style, containing articles by Hubbard and Foundation staff and details of courses, tape-recording and books available. Individuals within the Dianetic community rapidly became well known through letters, articles and personal stories in the group bulletins, and enthusiasts would make a point of visiting each other while in the neighbourhood of other Dianeticists on holiday or on business, often staying a while to try out each other's auditing techniques.

As the Foundations began training and certifying 'professional' auditors, other elements were added to the structure of the Dianetic community. Some trained auditors gravitated to leadership positions in the local amateur groups, virtually transforming the membership into a private clientele. In the Dianetics movement this was, however, fairly exceptional. Some set up entirely new private practices. Others were absorbed into the staff of the Foundations themselves. Some adopted a peripatetic form of practice, travelling around and engaging in a period of practice in one area before moving on to another.

A picture of how the professional practice of Dianetics was *ideally* envisaged is presented in one of the American newsletters.

A Dianeticist has his shingle out and a lady enters the waiting room. She has been troubled with her problems for some time now and feels that she may not be operating as optimum as she would like. Still she does not feel that a 'Nut Doctor' [psychiatrist] is the answer. She had heard that Dianetics has helped cases like hers, and after much mental hash and re-hash, she has decided to investigate. What's there to lose?

A pleasant girl, in a simple street dress, has received her, has asked the usual questions, and then instructed her to have a seat after telling her that the counselor would see her shortly. There is a buzzing and the receptionist rises and motions her to the door, politely shows her into the counselor's office and then leaves. The Auditor addresses the case in such a manner as to ascertain the problem and at the same time relax the patient as much as possible. There is no sales talk on Dianetics, no appeal at this time to assimilate its concepts. This would have nothing to do with the woman's problems. She has come to the Auditor for help as if he were a doctor, and in a sense that is exactly what he is. If he can help her he does, if not he lets her know and she goes her way. There is no converting, sales talk, or education. Treatment is what she wanted and treatment she should have, nothing more.[30]

Practitioners trained by the Foundation were eligible for Associate Membership in the HDRF, as were others interested in the practice of Dianetics, for a $15 annual fee. In return for this fee they were entitled to receive *The Dianetic Auditor's Bulletin*, the Foundation periodical publication. There was, however, little or no control over those who graduated from the Foundation courses. They received a certificate as an HDA (Hubbard Dianetic Auditor) and were henceforth entitled to practise their new-found profession wherever they chose. This was a source of concern to some board members of the Foundation, particularly Dr Joseph Winter.

Societal Reaction

While the response of the book-buying public rapidly placed Hubbard's book in the best-seller lists, it was not everywhere received with enthusiasm. Reviews by psychologists and psychiatrists were almost uniformly unfavourable. Rollo May objected to Hubbard's oversimplified monocausal determinism and regarded his grandiose promises as potentially harmful to mentally and emotionally troubled people.[31] Others objected to his repeated claims 'of exactitude and of scientific experimental approach, for which every trace of evidence is lacking', and suggested that patients might waste time in Dianetic therapy before seeing a doctor, time that could in severe cases prove fatal.[32]

More sympathetic reviewers suggested that Dianetics was harmless enough and might possibly even be of help to socially isolated individuals:

> The close relationship between the two people who 'audit' each other can become a bridge from the isolated person to the outside world. The person gets encouragement from another, no matter what kind, and thus achieves a feeling of connectedness with other people, and consequently succeeds where he has previously failed.[33]

The benefits of a sympathetic listener while the pre-clear ventilated his problems were recognized by some reviewers, who never-

theless remained concerned at the effects this might have in untrained hands in the case of severe mental disorder.[34] Although
some of these reviews may have attracted people to Dianetics, it
was the view of informed Dianeticists that the reviews in the larger-
circulation periodicals and newspapers were generally so unfavourable that they had led many to fall away.

Apart from numerous marginal, limited and quasi-medical converts, Dianetics was received coldly by the medical, psychiatric
and psychological professions. Dr Gregory Zilboorg publicly
attacked Dianetics before a forum at the New York Academy of
Medicine,[35] and the American Psychological Association's resolution calling on psychologists not to employ Dianetic techniques
in therapy was widely reported.[36]

Winter, as medical director of the first Foundation, attempted
to interest his colleagues in Dianetics, but with little success. A
meeting was arranged in Washington DC, at which Hubbard
lectured to a group of 'psychiatrists, educators and lay people'.
Winter comments on this meeting:

> I did not feel that the Washington venture was a successful one
> – at least, not from the medical point of view. It was noteworthy
> that most of the people whose interest in dianetics had been
> augmented by this presentation were members of the laity,
> rather than the profession, and I thought that I could detect in
> their attitudes the fervor of the convert, rather than the cool,
> objective interest of the scientist. The professional people evi-
> denced an interest in the philosophy of dianetics; their interest
> was repelled however, by the manner of presentation of the
> subject, especially the unwarranted implication that it was
> necessary to repudiate one's previous beliefs before accepting
> dianetics.[37]

Dr Morris Fishbein, a spokesman for the American Medical Association, was widely reported for his castigation of Dianetics as yet
another 'mind-healing cult'.[38]

Some sectors of the medical profession clearly took the view that
there was a need for more active steps to be taken to deal with what

was seen by some doctors as a form of quackery. In January 1951, it was reported in a *Bulletin* of the Elizabeth Foundation that: 'Because no teaching license was ever procured for New Jersey despite reports that it had been in June, Elizabeth is under suit from the State for teaching without a license.'[39] The New Jersey Board of Medical Examiners had initiated an injunction against the Elizabeth Foundation, later vacated, for conducting a school of medicine without a licence. It was almost certainly as a result of the publicity given to this action that creditors of the Foundation began to demand settlement, leading to reorganization and centralization of the Foundation at Wichita.

Possibly as a result of this response from the established therapeutic professions, Hubbard has since demonstrated a marked antagonism to medical practitioners, and to psychiatrists in particular. He brushed aside all criticism, attributing it to the ignorance of the critics and their vested interests in the income and the prestige of practices threatened by Dianetics; to their engramic condition; and to professional incompetence.

The Decline of Dianetics

The major external cause of the Dianetics decline was the fall-off in numbers of new recruits which led in turn to a financial crisis. The central organizations of Dianetics were poorly administered. Hubbard was lecturing in various parts of the country and commuting between Los Angeles and New York during late 1950 and early 1951, giving little direction to either of these Foundations in day-to-day administration, and progressively alienating other board members by his practice of initiating developments without consulting them, and by what some of them viewed as his increasingly evident authoritarianism.

Large numbers of staff were recruited in the early months, without adequate supervision. Foundation income was expended on the assumption that the Dianetics boom would long continue. However, by the beginning of 1951 applications for training and therapy began to drop off and income correspondingly fell. In part, as we have argued, the decline in numbers of new recruits to

Foundation services was precipitated by attacks on Dianetics by doctors and psychiatrists in the press and scathing reviews of Hubbard's book. Recruitment may also, to some extent, have been affected by adverse publicity resulting from a divorce action in which Hubbard was involved. In particular, however, the decline in numbers was due to the failure of Dianetics to live up to its promise in the eyes of its early mass public. The 'clear' who would emerge after only twenty hours of auditing had not made his appearance, and many individuals who had been working at the technique found their cases had improved little or not at all, and gave up.

Yet another reason for attrition was the presentation of Dianetics as a psychotherapy. Whatever their feelings about the state of 'clear', many people had gone into Dianetics to solve relatively specific problems of illness or psychological handicap. Whether through spontaneous remission, the hope given them by Dianetics, the attention they received as pre-clears, or the therapeutic validity of the practice, a number had felt improved in consequence. Having secured what they had wanted from Dianetics, some discontinued involvement.

The Elizabeth Foundation moved towards a financial crisis. Hubbard saw the need to take some action to cope with this situation, but Joseph Winter and Hubbard's publisher resigned from the Board of Directors in October 1950. C. Parker Morgan resigned in January 1951 and John W. Campbell in March 1951. Creditors began to demand payment of their bills and Hubbard, faced with financial disaster and threats of commitment by his wife Sara during the divorce action, resigned in April 1951 and went to Cuba.

Don Purcell, a Wichita businessman, offered to assist the Foundation out of its difficulties. The Foundation was centralized and its assets moved to Wichita, Kansas, in April/May 1951, where Purcell made available funds and a building. Purcell became President of the Foundation and Hubbard its Vice-President and Chairman of the Board of Directors on his return from Cuba. The other branches were closed down and the number of staff drastically reduced. The New Jersey creditors, however, pressed for settlement of the Elizabeth Foundation's debts, and a court decision declared the Kansas operation its successor and liable for its debts. A receiver was appointed. A compromise settlement of the claims was negotiated, but new claims were filed by other creditors.

Hubbard broke with his colleagues (who then declared the Foundation bankrupt) and moved to Phoenix, Arizona, where he publicized new developments in his theory and practice, which he called Scientology. Scientology, far from being a lay psychotherapy, developed progressively into a highly professionalized religious philosophy, and was shortly incorporated as a church.

Internal Sources of Crisis

The crisis that overtook Dianetics also emerged as the resolution of a variety of strains and conflicts within the Dianetics community, which existed between Hubbard and other leaders, between Hubbard's desire for a strong central organization and the amateur groups keen to retain their independence, and between Hubbard and other innovators of theory and practice.

The break between Hubbard and Purcell was the culmination of a series of strains in their relationship and even earlier difficulties with other co-leaders of the movement. Winter, for example, had broken with Hubbard over a number of issues, of which the financial precariousness of the Elizabeth Foundation was only one. Firstly, Winter said that he had found

> ... a difference between the ideals inherent within the dianetic hypothesis and the actions of the Foundation in its ostensible efforts to carry out these ideals. The ideals of dianetics, as I saw them, included non-authoritarianism and a flexibility of approach; they did not exclude the realization that this hypothesis might not be absolutely perfect. The ideals of dianetics continued to be given lip-service, but I could see a definite disparity between ideals and actualities.[40]

He had growing doubts about the possibility of achieving the state of 'clear', and was concerned at the extent to which the effects of Dianetic therapy were simply the result of suggestion. He felt that the effect of the techniques might not always be beneficial to the pre-clear, and indeed might sometimes be positively dangerous in the hands of poorly-trained auditors without adequate medical knowledge. The increasing disparagement of 'the medical profession and the efforts of previous workers in the field of mental health' disturbed him, as well as the absence of scientific research – for the purpose of which the Foundation had supposedly been established.[41] The research which was being conducted was directed to 'investigating the possible therapeutic benefits of "recalling" the circumstances of deaths in previous incarnations'.[42] Winter did not regard this concern with 'past-lives' (which was to achieve much greater prominence in Scientology) as likely to increase the acceptability of Dianetics to the medical profession. Finally, he objected to the uncontrolled administration of a vitamin and glutamic acid compound familiarly known as 'Guk', as an aid to therapy. His protests concerning these matters met with a sharp rebuff, 'and I was led to infer that I was acting as a deterrent to the progress of the Foundation'.[43] He therefore resigned from the Foundation to establish a private psychotherapy practice in Manhattan, where he combined Dianetics with psychoanalysis and General Semantics.

John W. Campbell in retrospect also criticized what he viewed as the increasing dogmatism and authoritarianism of Hubbard.[44] The relationship between Hubbard and Purcell followed a similar pattern. After a short period of co-operation, Hubbard began to feel that Purcell was constraining his control over the development of Dianetics. Purcell attempted to establish the Foundation on what he saw as a sound business footing, but Hubbard rapidly began generating new techniques faster than students could be trained in them. More money was being spent than was being earned as experimentation continued with vitamin compounds and later started with electropsychometers.

When Purcell insisted that expenditure be reduced to meet income, Hubbard began initiating independent fund-raising schemes which came to be a source of embarrassment to other Foundation directors, and a source of further expense.[45] Finally,

Hubbard insisted on pursuing the matter of past-lives in spite of the protests of other leaders of the Dianetics movement, including Purcell. Like Winter and Campbell before him, Purcell found Hubbard attempting to secure sole authority: 'Ron's motive has always been to limit Dianetics to the Authority of his teachings. Anyone who has the affrontry [*sic*] to suggest that others besides Ron could contribute creatively to the work must be inhibited.'[46]

While Hubbard was facing challenges to his authority at the centre of the movement in the Foundations, challenges were also appearing from the grass roots. These took a number of forms. The dispersed amateur groups which formed the main active body of support for Dianetics exhibited a considerable independence. They tended to view with suspicion attempts to organize more than a loose central organization and the possibility of the infringement of their autonomy. The attitude most prominent in the publications was one of an independent, democratic individualism. One description of the movement by a Dianeticist represented it as 'processing of ordinary cases by ordinary people. It means ordinary people getting together for study and practice. It means little groups of dianeticists up and down the country.'[47] While others saw Dianetics as moving towards a professional rather than an amateur basis, they retained a preference for a democratic form of organization.

Hostility was frequently expressed in the independent Dianetics literature against 'authorities' of any kind. As early as mid 1951, at the time of the much publicized divorce case between Hubbard and his second wife Sara, it was argued that the movement could well proceed without Ron Hubbard, and on the occasion of the split between Hubbard and the Wichita Foundation, a section of the movement took the view that there was no reason to identify Dianetics with Hubbard, and that as

Physics is a science independent of Newton; Dianetics is a science independent of Hubbard. . . . Hubbard is not the only original thinker in Dianetics – many others are thinking and producing ideas, some, elucidations of Hubbard's ideas, some ideas that Hubbard has never mentioned.[48]

Dianetics would progress, they argued, 'with or without Hubbard'. This attitude of independence and individualism led many practitioners to generate new Dianetic techniques and theoretical rationales. Some felt their innovations to be so far-reaching as to have become a completely new practice deserving a separate name and recognition, and set up 'Institutes', 'Schools' and 'Foundations' of their own to propagate the practice. This diversification was deplored by some Dianeticists, but applauded by others. Some innovators, while admitting their basis in Dianetics, often believed that their own developments had greatly surpassed those of Hubbard. One former Dianeticist who established his own Foundation even had the temerity to offer for sale a book entitled *Dianetics Perfected*. Others, while not extensively developing independent theories and procedures, eclectically combined Hubbardian theory and practice with those of other psychological and philosophical schools: Carbon Dioxide Therapy, New Thought affirmations, nutritional regimes, Orgone Therapy, etc.[49]

A widely prevailing view was that any theory or technique which could help gain the ends sought through Dianetics should be employed. Some practitioners became extremely eclectic, one describing a technique derived from 'Krishnamurti, Henshaw Ward, Gestalt Therapy, Analytical Procedure, and Karen Horney'.[50] A few moved towards more occult realms; one group even began delving into alchemy in order to create gold.

For many others, however, the direction in which they wished Dianetics to proceed was towards a rapprochement with the medical and psychological professions. They viewed Dianetics explicitly as a form of psychotherapy; tended to reject the occult and spiritual aspects of the theory that were developing in Hubbard's thinking, such as the idea of past-lives; and restricted themselves to the form of practice presented in Hubbard's early Dianetic works. The shift in Hubbard's later publications towards more mechanistic procedures of rote processing on the basis of prepared lists of auditing questions and commands, alienated them further.

Some of those who possessed a model of Dianetics as a therapeutic art advocated the assimiliation of elements of orthodox healing theory and practice:

> . . . we should not hesitate to carefully examine and integrate
> into Dianetics, where applicable, any and all of the techniques
> which are in common use in psychological and psychiatric
> practice. Certainly these practices work to a certain extent; in
> so far as they are useful and safe, they will have to be integrated
> into Dianetics eventually. If they are not, then Dianetics will
> not develop into the complete, well-rounded and comprehen-
> sive science of the mind that it now *potentially* is.[51]

Finally, a number expressed a commitment to the notion of
Dianetics as a science, independent of the medical or psychological
professions, but rejected Hubbard's occult developments.

All such views were reported in the independent Dianetics
media. New techniques were presented and new theories discussed
with considerable tolerance, reflecting the tolerance and eclectic-
ism of many of their readers and correspondents. Hubbard did not
regard such views and developments favourably, however. From
the time of the Elizabeth Foundation he had called developments
of Dianetic techniques which he did not sponsor 'Black Dianetics',
and declared the mixing of Dianetics with some other therapy to
be the source of many problems with students and pre-clears.

The Self-improvement and Healing Cults

Dianetics has a place in a continuing tradition of self-improvement
movements in the recent history of the United States. Enormously
accelerated social mobility and an ideology of individual achievement led to the emergence of a concern for infallible techniques
that would ensure success for the mobility-oriented. This was a
particularly pressing concern for those who had failed in, or failed
to gain access to, the major channels of mobility in modern industrial societies, the institutions of higher education. The late nineteenth and early twentieth centuries saw the appearance of various
movements and organizations which offered access to advanced,
occult, metaphysical, or otherwise esoteric knowledge, and some

which, more cynically, merely offered certification that access to such knowledge or training had been obtained. The 'diploma-mill' became an established, if derogated, institution. Movements such as New Thought suggested that prosperity and success were available to everyone. The use of a few simple techniques would enable anyone to overcome the limitations which he believed held him back.[52]

Dianetics also found a place in the continuing tradition of healing movements in the United States. Indeed, the two traditions overlapped to a very high degree, movements within this domain offering both healing and self-improvement, and certifying 'professional' competence in the practices purveyed.[53] The development of science, particularly medical science, during the nineteenth century, led, John Lee has argued, to increased expectations regarding physical health and comfort. These expectations were in excess of what medicine could actually achieve.

> The great breakthroughs in medical research by Lister, Pasteur and many others had created a new level of expectation that medicine could defeat man's age-old enemies of pain and disease. New accomplishments in engineering, agriculture and public sanitation brought the hope of a healthier, more comfortable life to the lowest citizen. But it was a long time after many of these advances became theoretically possible that they were actually realized for the average person. . . .[54]

> From about 1860 to at least 1900, in the experience of all but the wealthier classes, there was a very real gap between the ultimate promise and the actual performance in medicine and public health measures. The medieval resignation to disease and pain was gone, but the modern means of accomplishing general health and well-being for the whole population were not yet fully mobilized.[55]

The new healing movements such as Christian Science and New Thought offered a means of overcoming this gap between expectation and performance in the realm of physical healing. While medicine became increasingly specialized and compartmentalized and allopathic medicine directed attention to the disease rather than the individual, leading to a depersonalization of the practitioner-client relationship, the new healing movements retained a personal orientation, a concern for the 'whole man'.[56] Hence it has been argued that the role of the practitioner in such movements is closer to that of the psychotherapist than of the medical practitioner.[57] The therapeutic success claimed by such movements is often attributed to mistaken diagnosis, the 'placebo effect', spontaneous remission, and the mobilization of the patient's expectation of healing.[58] This expectation can be heightened and directed by the therapist in subtle, and often unconscious ways, particularly if his own belief in the efficacy of the practice is strongly held. The 'non-directive' or 'evocative' therapies employed afford a strong temptation to the therapist 'to induce the patient to express material that confirms his theories, because he can regard it as independent evidence for them; and the patient is induced to accept the therapist's formulations because he believes them to be his own.'[59] The therapist's very determination not to direct his patient may itself create 'an ambiguous situation that may increase the patient's suggestibility, and also arouse his anxiety and resentment, which ... may act as an incentive to change.'[60]

Even in the absence of conscious or unconscious 'coaching', the patient generally arrives for therapy with a fairly clear idea of the performance that he will be expected to produce. From material he has read, stories he has heard, or from generally available cultural stereotypes, he will construct an anticipatory image of the appropriate performance. In the case of Dianetics, reports of the practice were so widely published in newspapers and magazines that few pre-clears can have presented themselves for auditing without some knowledge of what experiences, were the session successful, they would undergo.

As, through the early twentieth century, medical practice became more competent to deal with physical illness, expectations of health and well-being became increasingly centred on the psychological domain and the difficulties of interpersonal relations. Movements like Christian Science and New Thought which had claimed efficacy in handling physical illness lost ground, while others arose offering psychological well-being, release of mental and emotional tensions, cures for psychosomatic and neurotic illness, techniques for releasing hidden inner abilities, and means of 'making friends and influencing people'. In such areas, science has yet achieved little concrete progress, and the market remains open to cultic groups offering knowledge and techniques produced by more mystical, occult, or pseudo-scientific means. Whatever the source of such knowledge the prestige of science has become such as to require that almost every new movement entering this field claim scientific legitimacy and authority, if by no other means than that of incorporating 'science' in its title.[61]

CONCLUSION

Dianetics struck a powerful resonance in the minds of many post-war Americans. It offered a rationale for failure in social mobility and in social interaction. It provided an explanation in terms of traumatic incidents in which the individual had been unwittingly involved, and thereby relieved him of responsibility for his failure. All the past mistakes, failures, and sources of guilt could be wiped out.[62] But most important of all, it offered a means of eradicating the persisting causes of his failure, and thus of attaining the level of achievement to which he aspired. In a status-striving age it provided a means of improving the individual's chances of status mobility. The theory of Dianetics assured its adherent that his 'true self', his conception of what he believed he was really capable of achieving, was indeed as he conceived it. It reaffirmed this idealization of self and promised a means of eliminating the barriers to its fulfilment, of eradicating the gap between his 'true self' and the identity that was typically confirmed in social interaction. Moreover, Dianetics provided a means of understanding not only oneself, but also of understanding others, a way of categorizing and accounting for their behaviour, and a guide to appropriate responses.

Dianetics seems to have been seen as an acceptable and legitimate solution to the problems with which recruits were faced for two reasons: they had either tried alternative systems of belief and practice and found them unsuccessful; or, they had rejected such alternative systems as inappropriate to their situation. Many of those interviewed claimed an acquaintance with the literature of psychology, and expressed dissatisfaction with it. Psychology as far as they could see, in the 1940s, was split between behaviourism and psychoanalysis. Behaviourist psychology seemed to have little or no relevance to man in general and no solution to their problems in particular. Psychoanalysis, while addressing many of the problems which they faced and offering solutions to them, had two major drawbacks. First, analysis seemed an inordinately lengthy process, often lasting several years. Second, it was too expensive for most to consider it a practical proposition.

Those who were suffering physical ills or disabilities had generally tried medical means of overcoming them, but had found little satisfaction from medical professionals, few of whom recognized the essentially psychological or social basis of many of the complaints presented to them. Ill-equipped through lack of training to cope with the needs of such patients, they resorted to pharmacological or surgical treatments which, while successful in some cases, left others feeling the need for a treatment practice which took greater account of man as a whole. Others, suffering from chronic illnesses for which medical treatment had proved unsuccessful or from illnesses for which effective therapeutic interventions had not yet been discovered, had exhausted all the resources that orthodox medicine could offer. In the case of those suffering both physical and mental problems, the individuals concerned had generally sought solutions in a variety of other therapeutic practices before they came in contact with Dianetics.

Bureaucratization and the scale of modern urban society produce a context in which many individuals experience a lack of control over their destiny and environment, a sense of being moved and constrained by forces beyond their control. Many of those who did not conceptualize their situation in medical or psychological terms experienced the world in which they lived as more or less unpredictable, chaotic, or meaningless. They sought some means of greater control over their environment and their reactions to it. Related to this, a small proportion were engaged in therapeutic work of a limited or marginal kind, and saw considerable limitations in the tools they had available. A further small proportion claimed a simple intellectual curiosity, which had earlier led to other systems of self-improvement, metaphysics or occult knowledge.

While science held great promise, having delivered technological 'cargo', and having proved a powerful tool in the improvement of material conditions, it had done little to solve perennial and increasing problems of psychological well-being, to provide cures for certain forms of illness, or to equip man better to cope with his social environment. Dianetics followers tended to conceptualize appropriate solutions to such problems as being 'scientific' in form. Their conception of science was, however, a lay conception (albeit a lay conception which has from time to time been offered as an academic account in the form of Pragmatism). It was technological and instrumental in form. What constituted a science was a body of knowledge which appeared to explain some set of phenomena in a rational and consistent way, and which provided a means of intervening in the processes involved so as to achieve successful or desired outcomes. Their test of standing of any body of knowledge was: Does it work, i.e. do interventions of the prescribed form issue in desired outcomes? When, after a Dianetic session they felt better than before, they concluded that it worked.

They tended to expect that new and important scientific developments would appear through media or institutions marginal to the scientific community. Their conception of this community was one of an elitist group with vested interests in the promotion of particular theories and practices, unwilling to accommodate new ideas or even to give them a fair hearing. Hence the innovator would generally need to find a more marginal institutional base in order to get his revolutionary new thoughts heard.

Dianeticists appear to have held a belief in the *immanence of knowledge*; that it was freely available and anyone who applied himself might expect to secure radically new or deeper insights into the nature of the world. They also held a belief in the *elitism of science*; that scientists had arrived at their own views to which they were unwilling to permit any radical challenge. Since orthodox science was so conservative on this account, the intellectually curious might seek truth in less orthodox realms: metaphysical or occult groups, marginal healing, philosophical or psychological movements, or science fiction. Science fiction provided all that science lacked, filling in the lacunae of scientific knowledge or competence with fictional or speculative detail, and blurring the distinction between the empirical and the conceivable. Converts to Dianetics were mobilized to accept an unorthodox system of belief and practice by the urgency of their need, which orthodox systems had been unable to supply, or by a conviction that radical developments in knowledge were to be anticipated outside the domain of the institutions of orthodoxy, which lacked the vision to generate them.

John W. Campbell, as editor of *Astounding Science Fiction,* was an influential figure in the science fiction world and its environs. His readership saw him as a man of vision, willing to give any idea a hearing. When Campbell gave his support to Dianetics, interest was aroused on the basis of his prestige and his enthusiastic acclaim of this new science of the mind. On publication of Hubbard's article in *Astounding,* the idea of 'clear', like that of 'flying saucer', became a kind of Rorschach blot,[63] a vague and amorphous image upon which any individual could impose his aspirations. Being clear, however Hubbard might define it, meant being able to do all those things which one currently could not do, and to which one aspired so desperately.

Despite its initial impact, however, Dianetics foundered. It was to re-emerge later as a sub-component of Hubbard's much more successful and enduring movement, Scientology, but after reaching craze proportions in 1950, by 1952 it had effectively disappeared. Why had this happened?

Paradoxically, one reason for its demise would seem to have been the very popularity of the idea. Unlike chiropractic, osteopathy, etc., Dianetics was initially promoted as a lay psychotherapy which any two reasonably intelligent people could conduct on each other on the basis of Hubbard's book. Thousands bought the book, tried the practice, and then as readily abandoned it. Those who remained were fiercely jealous of their independence, resisting control by the central organizations, and innovating new theories and techniques, or eclectically combining Dianetics with other practices. Hence, it did not spread on the basis of trained professionals with a commitment to the practice as it had been revealed to them, carrying out their practice on an uninformed clientele to whom the mystery had not been revealed. Early in its history, therefore, Dianetics was riven by competing schools and factions which challenged not only each other's authority, but that of the movement's founder as well. Thus, the financial crisis which led to the bankruptcy of the central organization, and the crisis of authority resulting from the presentation of Dianetics as a lay psychotherapy in which any man could become an expert, combined to cause the movement's demise.

Hubbard was to demonstrate his understanding of the lessons implicit in these developments when he established Scientology. Scientology was organized from the outset in a highly centralized and authoritarian fashion, and practised on a professional basis. Its theory and method were only gradually revealed to those who displayed commitment to Hubbard and practised its techniques in a pure and unalloyed fashion. A rigorous system of social control emerged, and it was made clear to all followers that Hubbard was the sole source of new knowledge and interpretation of existing knowledge. It therefore succeeded in avoiding the fissiparousness which had overtaken Dianetics.

NOTES AND REFERENCES

1   This paper is based on extensive research into Dianetics and Scientology by the author. This research involved interviews with members and former members, the use of questionnaires, and the examination of a wide range of documentary sources. The study was funded in part by a generous grant from the Social Science Research Council. The paper draws heavily on my doctoral thesis *A Sociological Analysis of a Quasi-Religious Sect,*

Oxford University, 1974, and is more fully elaborated in Part II of my book *The Road to Total Freedom: A Sociological Analysis of Scientology,* Heinemann Educational Books, London, 1976, from which a substantial part of this paper is taken. I am grateful to Dr Bryan Wilson, for advice and encouragement throughout, and to Professor John Lee, for his comments on an earlier draft of this paper.

2   Walter I. Wardwell, 'A marginal professional role: the chiropractor', *Social Forces,* Vol. 30, March 1952, pp. 335-348; Idem, 'The reduction of strain in a marginal social role', *American Journal of Sociology,* Vol. 61, July 1955, pp. 16-25; Thomas McCorkle, 'Chiropractic: a deviant theory of disease and treatment in contemporary western culture', *Human Organisation,* Vol. 20, Spring 1961, pp. 20-23.

3   Harold D. McDowell, *Osteopathy: A Study of a Semi-Orthodox Healing Agency and the Recruitment of its Clientele,* unpublished MA Thesis, University of Chicago, 1950.

4   R. W. England, 'Some aspects of Christian Science as reflected in letters of testimony', *American Journal of Sociology,* Vol. 59, No. 5, 1954, pp. 448-453; Walter I. Wardwell, 'Christian Science Healing', *Journal for the Scientific Study of Religion,* Vol. 4, No. 2, 1965, pp. 175-181; Arthur E. Nudelman and Barbara E. Nudelman, 'Health and illness behavior of Christian Scientists', *Social Science and Medicine,* Vol. 6, 1972, pp. 253-262; Bryan R. Wilson, *Sects and Society,* Heinemann, London, 1961.

5   E.g.: J. E. Hulett, 'The Kenny healing cult: preliminary analysis of leadership and patterns of interaction', *American Sociological Review,* Vol. 10, 1945, pp. 364-372; Vieda Skultans, *Intimacy and Ritual,* Routledge, London, 1974; E. T. Cassee, 'Deviant illness behavior: patients of mesmerists', *Social Science and Medicine,* Vol. 3, 1970, pp. 389-396. There is, of course, an extensive literature on healers in non-industrial nations, but only a very limited literature on unorthodox healers in industrial nations.

6   John W. Campbell, 'In times to come', *Astounding Science Fiction,* Vol. 44, No. 4, December 1949, p. 80.

7   L. Ron Hubbard, 'Dianetics: the evolution of a science', *Astounding Science Fiction,* Vol. 45, No. 3, May 1950, pp. 43-87. It was soon followed by a number of further articles in this magazine, in which Hubbard elaborated other aspects of the theory and practice of Dianetics.

8   L. Ron Hubbard, *Dianetics: The Modern Science of Mental Health,* Hermitage House, New York, 1950. All references are to the edition published by the Hubbard College of Scientology, East Grinstead, 1968.

9   Ibid.; and L. Ron Hubbard, 'Dianetics: the evolution of a science', op. cit.

10   L. Ron Hubbard, *Dianetics: The Modern Science of Mental Health,* op. cit., p. 314.

11   Ibid., p. 262.

12   Ibid., p. 211.

13   L. Ron Hubbard, *Dianetics: the Evolution of a Science,* Publications

Organisation, World Wide, 1968, p. 76. This book is a modified version of Hubbard's *Astounding* article.

14 L. Ron Hubbard, *Dianetics: The Modern Science of Mental Health,* op. cit., p. 159.

15 Ibid., p. 200.

16 Ibid., p. 202.

17 Ibid., p. 92.

18 Ibid., p. 92.

19 Ibid., p. 93.

20 L. Ron Hubbard, *Self-Analysis in Dianetics,* Derricke Ridgway, London, 1952, p. 32.

21 Introduction to L. Ron Hubbard, *Dianetics: The Modern Science of Mental Health,* op. cit., p. xxiii.

22 The demographic data derive primarily from a survey conducted by a Dianetic newsletter and reported in *The Dianews,* Vol. 1, No. 23, 15 June, 1952. The motivational data derive from my own documentary analysis, interviews and questionnaires.

23 Dalmyra Ibanez *et al, Dianetic Processing: A Brief Survey of Research Projects and Preliminary Results,* Hubbard Research Foundation, Elizabeth, New Jersey, 1951, pp. 34-35.

24 Interview.

25 Letter from the Australian Psychology Centre, *Dianotes,* Vol. 1, Nos. 9-10, March-April, 1952, p. 8.

26 Correspondent, *The Aberree,* Vol. 2, No. 4, July-August 1955.

27 Joseph A. Winter, *A Doctor's Report on Dianetics: Theory and Therapy,* Julian Press, New York, 1951, pp. 7-8.

28 Ibid., p. 6.

29 Advertisement in *Astounding,* Vol. 46, No. 3, November 1950, back cover.

30 *Dianotes,* Vol. 1, No. 12, June-July 1952, p. 2.

31 Rollo May, 'How to back-track and get ahead', *New York Times Book Review,* 2 July, 1950.

32 Martin Gumpert, 'The dianetics craze', *New Republic,* No. 132, 14 August, 1950, pp. 20-21.

33 Willard Beecher and Calder Willingham, 'Boiled engrams', *American Mercury,* No. 73, August 1951, p. 80.

34 Anonymous, 'Dianetics', *Consumer Reports,* August 1951, pp. 378-380.

35 'Dr Zilborg attacks dianetics', *New York Times,* 30 March, 1951, p. 15.

36 'Psychologists act against Dianetics', *New York Times,* 9 September, 1950, p. 7.

37 Winter, op. cit., pp. 29-30.

38 'Poor man's psychoanalysis', *Newsweek,* 16 October, 1950, pp. 58-59.

39 *Bulletin,* 21 January, 1951; *The Dianamic,* No. 13, 8 February, 1951, p. 3.

40 Winter, op. cit., p. 30.

41 Ibid., p. 40.

42 Ibid., p. 189.

43 Ibid., p. 190.

44 John W. Campbell, 'Letter' in *The Arc Light,* No. 25, May 1952, pp. 6-8.

45 The details of these schemes are discussed in Roy Wallis, *The Road to Total Freedom,* op. cit.

46 *Dianetics Today,* Vol. 3, No. 1, January 1954.

47 *The Dianeticist,* Vol. 1, April 1952, p. 3.

48 *Dianews,* Vol. 1, No. 22, 31 May, 1951, p. 2.

49 *Dianotes,* Vol. 3, No. 26, November 1953; *Dianotes,* Vol. 4, No. 45, June 1955, p. 6; *The Arc Light,* 26 January, 1952.

50 *Dianotes,* Vol. 3, No. 28, January 1954, p. 5.

51 *Introductory Bulletin of the Central Pennsylvania Dianetic Group,* August 1951, pp. 2-3.

52 A. W. Griswold, 'New Thought: a cult of success', *American Journal of Sociology,* Vol. 40, No. 3, 1934, pp. 308-318.

53 Lee R. Steiner, *Where Do People Take Their Troubles?,* Houghton Mifflin, Boston, Mass., 1945.

54 John A. Lee, *Sectarian Healers and Hypnotherapy,* Queen's Printer, Toronto, 1970, p. 7.

55 Ibid.

56 Ibid., p. 5.

57 R. W. England, 'Some aspects of Christian Science as reflected in letters of testimony', *American Journal of Sociology,* op. cit.

58 Ibid.; E. T. Cassee, 'Deviant illness behavior: patients of mesmerists', op. cit.; Jerome D. Frank, *Persuasion and Healing,* Johns Hopkins Press, Baltimore, Maryland, 1961.

59 Frank, op. cit., p. 168.

60 Ibid.

61 Science of Mind; Christian Science: the Science of Creative Intelligence; *Dianetics: The Modern Science of Mental Health.*

62 Helen O'Brien, *Dianetics in Limbo,* Whitmore Publishing Co., Philadelphia, Pennsylvania, 1966, p. 72.

63 See: H. Taylor Buckner, 'The flying saucerians, a lingering cult', *New Society,* 9 September, 1965.

Gillian Allen and Roy Wallis

6

Pentecostalists as a Medical Minority

The socially constructed world is an ordering of experience. A meaningful order, or *nomos* in Peter Berger's[1] terminology, is imposed upon the discrete experiences and meanings of individuals. This ordering activity is a collective enterprise. Meanings are shared and thus acquire an 'objective' character. Common interpretations of experience come to be seen as 'objective knowledge' by the members of a society. This paper is concerned with the 'objective knowledge' about the causation and cure of illness, and their religious legitimations for suffering in general, shared by members of a small congregation of a Pentecostal church, the Assemblies of God, in a Scottish city.

THE ASSEMBLIES OF GOD AS A RELIGIOUS SECT

The Assemblies' basic doctrines are generally similar to the teachings of other evangelical movements. The Bible is accepted as the literally true and inspired Word of God, 'the Infallible and All-Sufficient Rule for Faith and Practice';[2] all other sources of knowledge are suspect. The doctrine of the Second Coming of Christ is formally adhered to, but it is not now a central feature of Pentecostal preaching. The essential evangelical doctrine of individual guilt for sin, and the need to obtain redemption through Christ's substitutionary atoning death, are continually emphasized. Salvation can be won when the individual's sense of guilt for sin leads him to 'accept Jesus Christ as his personal saviour' who bears his

110

sins, and was crucified for them. It is the subjective experience of 'asking Jesus to come into your heart', and the subsequent gratitude for the relief of guilt and the promise of eternal life which charges the Assemblies' meetings with emotion. It is the experience of salvation and of a developing personal relationship with God that is the crucial aspect of their religion for Assembly members. Doctrine is not so important.

Pentecostalists are distinctive in their belief in the 'baptism of the Holy Spirit' as a reality for present-day believers as much as for the early disciples on the day of Pentecost. Baptism in the Holy Spirit is manifested by an emotional reaction and the receipt of 'spiritual gifts' which include the gifts of speaking in 'divers kinds of tongues', 'the working of miracles', and 'healing' (1 Cor. 12).

The Assemblies of God is the largest Pentecostal sect in the United Kingdom,[3] with an officially estimated 20,000 members in England and Wales and 500 members in Scotland in 1950. In the Scottish city considered here, Pentecostalists form a tiny minority of the population. The Assembly of God has about twenty adults and thirteen children attending regularly (0.02 per cent of the city's population), with approximately another twenty occasional attenders. Including the Elim Foursquare and Apostolic Churches, Pentecostalism in this city claims less than 0.1 per cent of the population.

Membership in the Assembly is by proof of a conversion experience, baptism in water, and knowledge of the Assembly's twelve Fundamental Truths,[4] and entails obligations to attend regularly, contribute financially, live righteously, and try to be baptized in the Holy Spirit. Members who do not live up to these obligations can be expelled at the discretion of the pastor and elders, or of the whole meeting in serious cases. In fact this rarely happens, and social control is mainly informal.

Separation from the world is very limited. Physical or linguistic isolation is not practicable for a conversionist sect.[5] Endogamy is encouraged, but the in-group includes all 'born-again believers'. Insulation is mainly from popular leisure-time activities which are displaced by church-going; most Assembly members attend three to five times a week. Services are lively and quite entertaining in

themselves, however, with singing, clapping and banging tam-
bourines to modern hymn tunes. Self-expression is encouraged, the
more emotional the better, as long as it is within the narrowly prescribed range of themes, and couched in stereotyped religious
phraseology, except, of course, when 'the Spirit descends' and
spiritual expression breaks the bounds of language.

The Assembly is a community. 'We're like a family.' Members
refer to each other as 'brother' or 'sister', visit each other socially
and help each other, particularly in sickness. Control can therefore be exercised over a wide area of the member's life, and his
commitment must be fairly intense to endure it.

THE ASSEMBLY OF GOD AS A MEDICAL MINORITY

Theories of Illness Causation

What theories of illness causation are employed by members of the
Assembly of God? In general, the prevailing naturalistic explanations of disease are accepted. In answering questions about actual
illnesses they have had, causes were given as physical (germs,
viruses, cold and damp), or psychological (strain, worry, shock).
Their ideas about disease causation were not always strictly scientific, and could perhaps best be described as metaphysical in some
cases, due to their limited knowledge of scientific medicine rather
than to any belief in opposing theories.

However, some of the Assembly members also explained their
illnesses in spiritual terms. For 8 out of the 29 illnesses mentioned
(27 per cent), the question 'Do you think that it was just bad luck
that you got it?' was answered negatively, because it was seen as
God's will. Disease, in these cases, was explained in both scientific
and theistic terms, each operating at a different level. While the
immediate physical mechanism was explained scientifically, God
was believed to exercise ultimate control over these physical events.

More details of the supernatural theories of disease causation
held by the Pentecostalists were obtained in answer to questions
about the causes of disease in general, rather than their own

specific illnesses. The questions were: 'You've probably heard people arguing over why God allows people to suffer, even saved Christians; what do you think about it?'; 'Do you think God still sends sickness as a punishment for sin, like he did in the Old Testament?'; and 'Is disease ever caused by the Devil?' The theories of disease causation revealed in their answers can be classified under *demonic, theistic* and *metaphysical* headings.

Demonic theories. Sixteen out of the 20 Assembly members thought that disease could be caused by the Devil; only one heretic asserted 'Disease is caused by germs'! Assembly members accept a strict dualism between God and the Devil: 'A non-Christian life is a life with the Devil – there's no half-way house.' Since God is the source of goodness, it follows that 'all badness ultimately comes from the Devil – the source of evil,' so it must usually be the Devil who sends illness because, as one person expressed it, 'I can't see why the Lord would, unless someone was backsliding and the Lord wanted to draw them closer to him.'

The Deacon of the Assembly categorized the ways the Devil can cause disease into 'direct' and 'indirect'. He can cause disease directly as he did to Job: 'So went Satan forth from the presence of the Lord, and smote Job with sore boils from the sole of his foot unto his crown.' (Job 2:7) Or he can cause disease indirectly through sin, ignorance and apathy. One member of the Assembly, a health visitor, emphasized the role of the Devil in perpetuating ignorance: 'He blinds people to knowledge, particularly the rules of hygiene', and one old lady found that the Devil tempted her to adopt the sick role too readily: 'If you bucked up you could be better but the Devil says don't bother, just be ill.'

Whether or not the Devil causes disease is essentially an academic question for Assembly members. None of them mentioned the Devil as a causative agent in *actual* illnesses they had had, and some pointed out that 'you can't distinguish between diseases caused by the Devil, or allowed by God'.

'Possession by evil spirits', on the other hand, is actively used to explain not only mental illness but also some cases of dumbness, blindness and epilepsy. Demon possession is considered to be transferable by touch; and is exorcizable by prayer, by appealing to the

Spirit of God to overcome the evil spirits.

Theistic theories. Half the members of this congregation of the Assembly of God believed that God sometimes sends sickness as a punishment for sins. Illness might be a punishment for specific sins which provoked God's wrath, e.g. sexual misconduct: 'There was an unmarried couple who had a baby – it had spina bifida. This was a punishment for sin.' Or it might be a punishment for more general spiritual faults: 'If you get ill it makes you sit up and see what you're doing wrong – you're being disobedient somewhere.' It might sometimes be designed to lead the sinner back to right-eousness: 'God has to chastise us, but it's for our own good. It's done in love'; 'Sometimes people say it was through illness that they got converted'.

Disobedience to God was thought by some to result naturally in punishment, which might take the form of sickness: 'Just as a child, if it's disobedient, it has to be punished.' This belief that God can send illness as a punishment for sin is commonly held among fundamentalist Protestant groups.

The other half of the Assembly felt that God never sends illness as a punishment. They either believed, stressing God's role in the *healing* of sickness, that He does not deliberately send illness at all, or they believed that God sometimes sends illness, but not as a punishment. He might, for example, send illness to bring us closer to Him: 'The only way the Lord can get people to listen sometimes is to lay them on their back.' This view of illness causation is again in agreement with fundamentalist Christianity.

Metaphysical theories. A view of the relationship between sin and sickness emerged which was not mediated by God's direct intervention. It can therefore be categorized as metaphysical rather than theistic. There were two broad versions of this theory. Illness was seen as sometimes the result of sinful actions. Mental and physical illness was explained by this variant as the result of natural mechanisms, but the explanation was couched in moral-istic terms: 'Leading a loose, wicked life leads to illness as a natural result.' Disease might also result from the sin of a whole society: 'For example, Biafra. Man's sin leads to wars which lead to star-ving children.'[6]

An even less direct connection between sin and sickness can be observed in a variant of this theory in which sickness is seen as a concomitant of the sinful state of man, a result, therefore, of original sin. 'If there'd been no Fall, there'd be no sin and no sickness. Sickness is part of our heritage owing to the Fall.' One person accounted for the world-wide distribution of disease in these terms: 'We've brought it on ourselves through original sin and it's multiplied over the years, and through migration illness has been spread over the world.'

The two levels, natural and supernatural, of the theories of disease causation held by Assembly members fall within the competence of the medical and clerical professions respectively. The naturalistic theories, understood in scientific or quasi-scientific terms by Assembly members, do not conflict with those held by the medical profession. The supernatural theories do not differ markedly from those held by the Church of Scotland, particularly on its fundamentalist wing. Pentecostalists accept a similar conciliation of natural and supernatural causes as does the established church, though the supernatural is accredited with more power by Pentecostalists, e.g. in their belief in demons.

Theodicies

Among the questions to which illness gives rise is 'Why does illness exist?' Answers to this question have usually been given in religious terms, legitimating disease by reference to an ultimate reality in the context of which it appears more meaningful. The term *theodicy* encompasses such legitimations. Max Weber indentified three ideal-types of theodicy: dualism, karma, and predestination.[7] Theodicies of Assembly members were obtained in answer to the question 'You've probably heard people arguing over why God allows people to suffer, even saved Christians; what do you think about it?', from other questions about illness, and from sermons, prayers and Pentecostal publications.

Dualism. Dualist religion sees the world as a battleground where the forces of good struggle with the forces of evil. The material world and its imperfections are identified with the powers of darkness, as opposed to the powers of light of which the spirit of man forms a part. Man is thus actively engaged in the struggle on the side of the forces of order against the forces of chaos. Suffering is readily legitimated as being caused by the dark forces of chaos. Zoroastrianism is the prototypical dualist religion.

The doctrine of Satan as the power of evil acts as a dualistic theodicy. Although God is benevolent, suffering is believed to have entered the world through the malevolent forces of the Devil, which God could not prevent. Assembly members used dualistic legitimations for suffering when they subscribed to demonic theories of disease causation.

Karma. The law of karma, the inexorable law of cause and effect governing all ethical actions, explains our fortune in this life as the just deserts of past good and bad deeds, both in the present life and in previous existences. Assembly members employed forms of 'karmic' legitimation for suffering when they explained illness in metaphysical terms as the natural, just, and inevitable consequence of past sin.

Assembly members also offered legitimations of suffering more typical of the Judaeo-Christian tradition.

Predestination. The Judaeo-Christian tradition with its concept of God as benevolent, all-powerful and all-knowing, transcending the world that He created, encountered the problem of theodicy in its most acute form. How could the world's imperfections be reconciled with an ethical, omnipotent God? The Old Testament solution appears in the Book of Job, where in Weber's words, 'the omnipresent creator God must be envisaged as beyond all the ethical claims of his creatures, his counsels impervious to human comprehension. . . . The criteria of human justice are utterly inapplicable to his behaviour.'[8] Yet this submission is accompanied by the faith that somehow God's purposes are ultimately for the good of man: 'Though he slay me, yet will I trust in him,' declares Job. This attitude also characterizes Islam.

The most radical and systematic development of this stance of submission to an omnipotent deity occurs in the Calvinist doctrine of predestination. Man's powerlessness, contrasted with God's total power, leads logically to a complete determinism of human life, in this world and the next. An individual is predestined for heaven or hell and ethical behaviour cannot alter his fate. Human suffering is legitimated as part of God's inscrutable plan, and cannot be explained by the human concept of justice. The predestination theodicy is the logical outcome of a concept of God as transcendent and all-powerful, a solution made possible by denying God's benevolence.

Among Assembly members, none mentioned the *pure* predestination type of theodicy, though many had the attitude of submission found in Job. They legitimated suffering by saying: 'What seems unfair to us may only be because we can't see the future like God can'; or, similarly: 'There's always a purpose in it though we don't always see it.' This theodicy of submission fits in with the theistic theories of disease causation held by Assembly members. Whether God sent it as a punishment, or for the spiritual benefit of the patient, it is justified as being for the good of the sufferer in the long run. It may also be combined with demonic theories, as in the Book of Job, insofar as the Devil is used by God for some useful end.

Other solutions. Mitigations of this extreme sovereignty-submission theodicy have occurred within the Biblical tradition. One solution has been to project compensation for present misfortunes into a future revolution in this world, thereby making present suffering relatively less severe and integrating it into the nomos by extending the relevant time-scale. The interpretation of the doctrine of the Second Coming to mean the post-adventual establishment of the Kingdom of God on earth is characteristic of millennial sects in modern Protestantism, such as the Christadelphians and Jehovah's Witnesses.

A theodicy of future compensation in *this* world for present injustices is accepted by members of the Assembly of God in their belief in the imminence of the Second Coming, when the faithful will rule with Christ on earth. The suffering of believers will then be vindicated. As one of the congregation prayed: 'We who were the dust of the earth are going to reign with Him in glory.'

Present suffering may also be legitimated by the assurance of a just recompense in the *next* world.'For he that is least among you all, the same shall be great.' (Luke 9:48) Implied in this theodicy is the notion of the positive spiritual value of suffering for which otherworldly rewards can be expected.

The hope of compensation in the next world also legitimates present suffering for Assembly members. The Assemblies of God subscribe to a literal belief in Heaven and Hell. Their twelfth Fundamental Truth is: 'We believe in the bodily resurrection of all men, the everlasting conscious bliss of all who truly believe in our Lord Jesus Christ and that everlasting conscious punishment is the portion of all whose names are not written in the Book of Life.' Though salvation is by faith, this faith entails suffering: 'All that will live in godly Christ Jesus shall suffer persecution.' [9] This 'suffering for doing good' will, they hope, be rewarded in the next world.

Weber, surprisingly, omits any reference to Christology, the central Christian solution to the problem of suffering. The tension engendered by the discrepancy between a benevolent, omnipotent God and a suffering world was resolved, according to orthodox Christianity, by the crucifixion of Christ, by the suffering of a being who was both God and man. The suffering of man is legitimated by the suffering of God. Through its universality, suffering becomes a self-legitimating fact.

Christian suffering, then, by analogy with the crucifixion, may be justified by being considered ennobling. This attitude was very prominent among answers given by Assembly members. It was closely related to those theistic theories of disease causation in which God is believed to send illness in order to bring people closer to him. God is justified in sending illness, or in not preventing self-incurred illness, by the use made of it for the spiritual benefit of the sufferer. Illness may bring people 'closer to the Lord'; it may make them 'more compassionate'; or it may 'keep us humble'. Or suffering may be beneficial in preparing people for death: 'If you were always well you wouldn't want to leave this world, you'd be afraid of death. It prepares you for death.'

No theodicy. Many Assembly members, however, had no easily available answer to the question of why God allows suffering. Some said 'I don't know' or 'I hate this question'. The logical contradiction between an omnipotent, benevolent God and a world in which people suffer was felt acutely by some, who answered: 'It's difficult to say. I think it's more glorifying to God to be well,' or 'I like to think there's some divine purpose behind it for man's own good, but I can't quite accept it.' Others did not attempt to justify suffering, and just accepted that: 'We live in a world with germs where these things happen. There's no purpose behind it;' and that: 'God hasn't promised to save people from trouble, but to be with them in trouble.'

Theories of Treatment

The Assemblies of God do not explicitly accept or reject scientific theories of treatment. But they subscribe officially to a belief in divine healing. The eighth Fundamental Truth states that: 'We believe that the gifts of the Holy Spirit . . . have been set by God in the Church.' These include the 'gifts of healing' and the 'discerning of spirits' (1 Cor. 12:9-10). Divine healing can thus be a gift of the Holy Spirit, given to some people who have a special power to transmit the healing forces of the Holy Spirit. Similarly, the power to exorcize demons is believed to be God-given.

There is a second source of divine healing, mentioned in the tenth Fundamental Truth: 'We believe that deliverance from sickness, by Divine Healing, is provided for in the Atonement.' In the same way that Christ is believed to have been sacrificed vicariously for man's sin, by taking it on himself and relieving man of it, he is also thought, by Pentecostalists, to be able to take the sickness of believers. They quote Matthew 8:17: 'Himself [Christ] took our infirmities and bore our sicknesses.' Divine healing can, in theory, be obtained by anyone in the same way as salvation from sin, by faith in Christ. The procedure is laid down in James 5:14-16:

> Is any sick among you? Let him call for the elders of the church; and let them pray over him, anointing him with oil in the name of the Lord: And the prayer of faith shall save the sick, and the Lord shall raise him up; and if he have committed sins, they shall be forgiven him.

Confess your faults one to another, and pray one for another, that ye may be healed. The effectual fervent prayer of a righteous man availeth much.

The divine healing of James 5 rests on a holistic conception of health. The healing of sickness is a part of the healing or salvation of the whole man.

Neither the New Testament nor the Assembly of God Fundamental Truths distinguish between miraculous and non-miraculous healing. Members of the Assembly in fact use the term 'divine healing' in both senses, although it is most commonly used to mean healing by miraculous supernatural intervention in natural processes. In three quarters of the 26 cases of divine healing reported by Assembly members, the healing had occurred without medical treatment, or after the treatment had been perceived to be unsuccessful. Half of the recoveries were instantaneous or occurred within a few days. These healings were interpreted as miraculous.

But 'divine healing' was also applied in some cases where medical treatment and prayer had been used concurrently. This non-miraculous healing was considered divine insofar as God is believed to control all natural processes. One member explained: 'The Lord can heal you in any way, through tablets for example. . . . It all comes from the Lord if we are healed.'

While in this latter, non-miraculous sense 'divine healing' is perfectly compatible with dominant scientific notions of causation and treatment, miraculous 'divine healing' is not. The idea of supernatural healing is contrary to the basic assumptions of scientific medicine. The fact of remarkable physical cures following spiritual ministrations is not denied by the British Medical Association, but in their report on divine healing such cures are explained in psychological terms.[10]

Utilization Behaviour

In its beliefs about illness, the Assembly of God constitutes a medical cognitive minority. How far is the illness behaviour of members influenced by these beliefs?

Healing Procedures. Prayer for healing in the Assembly of God occurs at the end of normal services, when those who need healing, or help and advice, are asked 'to come out to the front'. There the pastor and elders perform the laying on of hands and sprinkling with holy oil, and pray simultaneously: 'Oh Lord, heal this woman! Yes, Lord! we know You can heal her.' The occasional case of demon possession is dealt with in a similar way, when the pastor or evangelist addresses the demon along these lines: 'Get out, foul demon! In the name of Jesus, leave her!' The pastor may visit and pray for the sick person at home or in hospital if he discovers someone is ill. Alternatively, prayer for the sick may occur at a distance, if the patient cannot attend church, for example; or via a material medium, such as a handkerchief, which is prayed over in church and taken to the patient in hospital.

Utilization. The use of divine healing in relation to orthodox medical services was investigated for both 'serious' and 'minor' illnesses. Data was collected for the most recent 'minor' illness like flu or a cold, and for a serious illness recalled by the respondent in answer to the question: 'Have you ever had a serious illness or accident?' It is likely that the selection of serious illnesses was biased towards those for which prayer had been used. Seventeen minor illnesses and 12 serious illnesses were reported.

The two help-seeking actions investigated were consulting the doctor, and being prayed for by the pastor in church or at home. Respondents were asked 'What happened from the time you first felt ill?'; 'Did you see the doctor about it?'; and 'Did you go out in church to get prayed for?' No Assembly members were private patients, so 'NHS' (National Health Service) will be used as synonymous with 'going to the doctor' and 'use of orthodox medical services'. 'Prayer' will refer to prayer by the pastor either in church or at home, not to private prayer, though in practice they are generally used together. Utilization of paramedical practitioners such as chemists, other unorthodox practitioners, and self-medication were not specifically investigated.

Factors influencing choice of pattern of utilization among Assembly members in the Scottish city were found to include the type of disorder, its seriousness and suddenness of onset, and its imputed cause. Greater variability in illness behaviour occurred for minor illnesses.[11] Six typical help-seeking careers could be distinguished:

i.   Divine healing as an *alternative* to the NHS.
ii. Divine healing as a *first resort* followed by use of NHS.
iii. Divine healing as a *supplement* to the NHS.
iv. Divine healing as a *last resort*.
v.   NHS only.
vi. Neither.

i. *Alternative.* Divine healing is used as an alternative to the NHS mainly in minor illnesses. Seven of the 17 minor illnesses reported were dealt with by prayer alone, whereas none of the serious illnesses were. Use of prayer as an alternative to the doctor was closely related to the perception of illness as spiritually caused. Prayer-only users when compared to doctor-only users more often attributed their illnesses to supernatural causes.

Some Assembly members see prayer for divine healing as a rule which ought to be followed 'in obedience to the Word of God'. Their faith in God as 'the Great Physician' is confirmed by their own experiences of divine healing. Sixteen of the 20 Pentecostalists interviewed claimed to have been divinely healed at some time in their lives, and past successes were given as reasons for current use of prayer. 'The Lord had healed my stomach a while back, so I assumed He could heal my sinusitis. But He didn't.'

Prayer may be expedient in some cases, when for instance, 'as far as I know doctors have no cure', or when 'The Lord could heal you much better than the doctor – you'd get a complete healing, whereas the doctor can't do much for you. They can't do much for varicose veins.' Divine healing may be used by some in an almost magical way, to avoid the pain and inconvenience involved in medical treatment. One woman chose prayer instead of the doctor because 'I was afraid he might tell me to rest and I can't afford to.' In minor illnesses, prayer is frequently used in conjunction with self-medication.

ii. *First resort.* Prayer for divine healing may be followed by a visit to the doctor if results are not forthcoming. This happened in 2 of the 12 serious illnesses reported. Although many feel that 'God should be the first resort', they recommend that 'after being prayed for two or three times and it doesn't work, go to the doctor'. How long a medical consultation should be postponed may depend on the theodicy held by the sick person: 'If you think God's trying your faith you'd hang on longer without getting the doctor.'

Whether God or the doctor is the first source of help depends partly on the type of illness; for faults in the mechanics of the body, such as broken bones, it is 'common sense to go to the doctor'; while some thought that for psychiatric illness or illness which would involve surgery, prayer should come first 'because the body is the Lord's'. Prayer may be used both to assist in making the decision whether to seek professional medical help, and as a form of treatment in its own right.

iii. *Supplement.* Prayer is used as a supplement to medical treatment particularly in serious illnesses. In 7 of the 12 serious illnesses reported, prayer for divine healing was used in conjunction with medical treatment, whereas this occurred in only 1 of the 17 minor illnesses. Typically, in serious illnesses of sudden onset, relatives or neighbours fetch the doctor immediately, and send for the pastor once the doctor has established the treatment regime.

Fetching the doctor is a procedure followed almost automatically in an emergency. About half the Assembly felt that even in less urgent cases they would use the medical services in the same way as anyone else, but pray as well. They rejected the way prayer was used almost magically by some Pentecostalists to achieve healing without any effort. They thought that 'God's willing to do His part, but we've got to do ours'. There was some criticism of those who refused medical treatment.

It was a common opinion that: 'There's nothing wrong with going to the doctor. God has given people the ability to be doctors and He's put medicine in the world.' Nevertheless, the doctor was generally regarded merely as an instrument of God, human and fallible, in whose knowledge and skills one could not place much faith. But because doctors are regarded as the instruments of God, the use of prayer plus doctor utilizes God's healing power most effectively. The Assembly's pianist expressed it as follows: 'God's methods are sometimes through men. Prayer makes the doctor's treatment successful.' Prayer, then, is often for 'divine healing' in the broader sense, including miraculous and non-miraculous healing.

The use of prayer and doctor together is seen as the most effecttive means of returning to complete health, physically, mentally and spiritually. The doctor may be used for physical treatment, but some Assembly members believe that a complete return to health involves a spiritual healing as well. In this way, their beliefs in the spiritual causation of disease, and the close relation of divine physical healing with spiritual salvation, influence their utilization behaviour.

iv. *Last resort.* Divine healing was occasionally used as a last resort after the medical services had failed to cure the disorder. Only 2 of the 12 serious illnesses and 1 of the 17 minor illnesses fell in this category. One woman with flu, for example, sent for the doctor first because she 'took it for granted that he would clear it up'. When the side effects of the drug he prescribed made her worse, she sent for the pastor to pray for her. A small minority of the Assembly (3 out of 20) thought that divine healing should *only* be used as a last resort.

v. *NHS only.* Prayer for divine healing was not used in 3 of the 12 serious illnesses and 8 of the 17 minor illnesses. Use of the health services only was closely related to the imputation of a purely physical cause. In none of these cases was a spiritual cause assigned to the disease. Lack of opportunity for going out for prayer limited its usefulness: 'You can always send for the doctor, but you can't always get to a meeting.' Prayer for the sick is a minor part of the pastor's role, so Assembly members were often reluctant to bother him.

vi. *Neither.* In 4 of the minor illnesses, neither the doctor nor the pastor was consulted because the complaints were 'too trivial'. Self-medication was used in these cases. 'A cold isn't a disease. Jesus Christ only healed diseases. When you can take a tablet yourself, I don't think it's out of place.' Similarly: 'I wouldn't class a cold as a sickness, so I wouldn't go to the doctor. I'd try all the treatments I could myself without bothering the doctor.'

The peculiarly Pentecostal beliefs about illness held in the Assembly of God are used by members in deciding on courses of help-seeking action. Belief in divine healing, as a theory of treatment, provides an alternative system to the health services, which may be employed in relation to the health services in the variety of ways described above. Theories of causation were found to be influential especially in minor illnesses, where belief in a spiritual cause was closely related to the use of prayer as an alternative to the doctor. In more serious illnesses, perception of a spiritual component in causation and cure resulted in the joint use of doctor and prayer. Theodicy was marginally influential in the choice of treatment system, when a medical consultation might be postponed if the illness was seen as a test of faith.

MAINTAINING A COGNITIVE MINORITY

Knowledge is constructed, maintained and transmitted through social interaction. Its continuing plausibility depends on the social support it receives. Its reality is supported by the conversations which include it as a background assumption. Systems of shared meaning require a social base to maintain them, what Peter Berger calls a 'plausibility structure'.

The maintenance of knowledge that contradicts the dominant interpretation of reality in a society requires particularly strong group support. This taken-for-granted character of the majority's knowledge and its refusal to accept the minority's knowledge as correct, or even as knowledge at all, weakens its credibility, and necessitates active, social measures to shore it up. Through the formation of a counter-community, in which conversations with the cognitive majority are limited, but those with fellow deviants are extensive, minority views can be protected.

Minority knowledge, threatened by the officially defined reality, requires explicit legitimations. Reasons why their knowledge is 'correct', and the official knowledge 'wrong', need explicit formulation.

Legitimations

Members of the Assembly of God, in their religious and medical beliefs and illness behaviour, are somewhat deviant from the surrounding population. But as a sect they have partly denominationalized, and as a medically unorthodox group they have compromised with the National Health Service. How do they legitimate their deviant illness behaviour in spite of the failures of divine healing and the successes of scientific medicine? And, conversely, how do they legitimate their accommodation to the dominant medical system in terms of their sectarian values?

Assembly members legitimate their use of divine healing by reference to God's 'command' in James 5: 'Is any sick among you? Let him call for the elders of the church.' Use of divine healing is further legitimated by its alleged advantages over scientific medicine. It is believed to give a 'complete' spiritual and physical cure. It is also believed to work where conventional medicine has failed. Members have a folklore of spectacular cures, some of which happened to themselves or their friends. It is the *interpretation* of a cure as divine that legitimates further prayer, and where the evidence is ambiguous it tends to be interpreted as supporting their belief in divine healing. Twelve of the 26 illnesses reported as divinely healed had not been diagnosed or treated by a doctor, yet they were cited as evidence of the success of divine healing, not as cases of natural recovery or spontaneous remission. Similarly, in 5 cases where medical treatment and prayer were used concurrently, the healing was interpreted as divine. Either the prayer rather than the medical treatment was alleged to be the effective agency, or 'divine healing' was being used in the non-miraculous sense. In some cases cures followed prayer where medical treatment had failed. Seven such cases were reported, of fairly serious conditions, possibly of partly psychological origin, such as duodenal and stomach ulcers, migraine, angina, thrombosis and a nervous breakdown. These healings were attributed by Assembly members to the power of God, rather than to any psychological effects of emotional healing services. Evidence for the fact of healing following prayer is solid enough for Assembly members to be able to legitimate its continuing use.

However, prayer often fails to save the sick. To investigate how the use of prayer is legitimated in the face of failure, Assembly members were asked: 'Have you ever prayed for divine healing but it didn't work? If yes: Why do you think it didn't work?' Fifteen of the 20 answered 'yes', but explained its failure to a non-believing interviewer in ways that did not threaten their fundamental beliefs. In their public rhetoric, at least, divine unresponsiveness does not lead to doubting the truth of James 5: 13-16, but to examining whether they are carrying out its instructions correctly. Thus the most commonly given reason for the failure of prayer was 'lack of faith'. Otherwise, legitimations for the failure of divine healing are those given for the occurrence of illness in the first place. The Job-type theodicy of submission to God's will: 'What we want at a particular time may not be what God wants to give us'; the Pauline theodicy of spiritual perfection through suffering; and the theodicy of illness as a 'chastening from God', were all mentioned. Two of the 5 who did not admit having had a prayer for healing answered, based their replies on a broader, non-miraculous definition of divine healing. Since 'all healing is divine', and they had eventually recovered, their use of prayer was justified. The failure of prayer to produce an immediate miracle does not invalidate Pentecostalists' belief in divine healing. Their justifications for its failures, and their readiness to interpret any improvement as a divine healing, help them legitimate their deviant medical beliefs.

The compromise of Assembly members with the 'world's' medical system requires legitimation in the light of God's 'command' of James 5. The usual justification given was that 'God's methods are sometimes through men'; 'God put doctors in the world and gave them their skills'. Once again, the non-miraculous sense of divine healing is used in an attempt to reconcile divine healing with scientific medicine, and thus to justify use of both.

Plausibility Structure

The deviant religious and medical knowledge held by Assembly members is maintained partly by cognitive devices such as explicit legitimations, and partly by social structural devices which ensure preferential association with fellow Pentecostalists. The typical sectarian mechanisms of a degree of separation from the 'world', and of high involvement in the deviant community are implemented by the Assembly of God in this Scottish city.

The relative separation of Assembly members from the 'world' arises from two sources: selection of isolated people to join the Assembly; and the active measures taken by the sect to keep itself apart.

It had been observed that people who join sects are often 'marginal men'[12] by reason of their relative deprivation in some area of life. Members of the Assembly were comparatively isolated from local neighbourhood and kinship networks. A high proportion were recent immigrants to the city. Ten of the 20 members interviewed had lived there for fewer than 5 years, compared with a probable 11 per cent for the population of the city as a whole, estimated from the 1960-61 rate of immigration.[13] Only 4 had lived there all their lives. Consequently members tended to lack the support of a kinship network. Ten of the Pentecostalists had no relatives other than their immediate family living in the city, while a further 2 had relatives but no contact with them. Nine of the 20 were single, widowed or divorced, and 5 of these lived completely on their own.

Thus members of the Assembly of God did tend to be 'marginal men'. Due to their recent arrival in the city they lacked local ties, and may have been further alienated by their cultural differences. Several shared the feelings of one man from Shetland who, although he had lived there for twenty years, confessed: 'I've never felt at home in [this city].'

However, Assembly members were not obviously 'deprived'. They were mainly in skilled manual or white collar occupations, or had been before they retired. Their homes were divided equally between the tenements in the older parts of the city, and the suburbs. They did not appear noticeably physically or mentally unwell, though they seem to have suffered from quite a number of psychosomatic conditions, including ulcers, nervous breakdowns and stammering. In this respect they contrasted with the occasional visitors to the meeting, who included a high proportion of noticeably mentally or physically handicapped people. While some may have joined the Assembly in response to their isolation in this city, 8 of the 20 were already Pentecostal before they came.

The measures taken by the Assembly to insulate its members from the 'world' were mainly directed against participation in popular leisure-time activities; church-going was substituted in their place. Some Pentecostalists reported severed relations with friends and kin because of their beliefs. But, as members of a conversionist sect with a duty to preach the gospel, interaction with unbelievers is inevitable, and they were all involved to some extent with non-Pentecostal friends at work, neighbours or relatives.

Their tenuous connections with the 'world' were counterbalanced by close connections with the Assembly community. Assembly members' deviant knowledge was continually reinforced in the frequent meetings they attended. Most went between three and five times a week normally, and more often during conversion campaigns. Some even spent their holidays at Pentecostal guest houses or youth camps. There was a lot of informal contact among them after meetings, and also mutual visiting unrelated to church activities.

Members were generally closely involved in the Pentecostal community. One of the principal benefits of membership was seen as 'fellowship', that is, friendship with people who were 'of like mind'. The single and widowed women, especially, emphasized this 'fellowship': 'You *belong* – you know there are people there who're your friends. You know there's someone you can go to. All my friends are members.' They also visited and 'encouraged one another', and 'in our Assembly of God people care for one another, much more so than in the Brethren'.

The Assembly of God may thus act as a functional alternative to neighbours and kin for some members, in providing entertainment, friendship and sometimes help, and in so doing may act as a plausibility structure for the maintenance of Pentecostal beliefs. As one member said: 'It's like a club. Their faith builds up your faith.'

Some evidence that involvement in the Assembly does help maintain belief in divine healing was obtained by examining intra-sect variations in attendance at meetings in relation to use of and belief in divine healing. Self-reported average weekly attendance was used as a measure of involvement in the Pentecostal com-munity. (Contacts with fellow Pentecostalists outside formal meet-ings were thus not taken into account – an omission which is likely to lead to an underestimate of the relationship between commun-ity involvement and beliefs.)

The findings showed that the higher his rate of attendance, the more likely was an Assembly member to place greater importance on prayer, as opposed to consulting the doctor, as a help-seeking action in illness. Attendance and belief were thus inter-related. Within the Assembly, a high rate of contact with fellow Pentecost-alists was conducive to the maintenance of Pentecostal beliefs about illness. But the relation is almost certainly not simply one-way. Attendance may reinforce belief but without initial belief there would be no attendance. Those whose faith is strongest would be most inclined to go to church. Attendance therefore pro-vides positive reinforcement for those who already believe.

Rate of attendance at meetings was also related to actual use of divine healing *vis-à-vis* the National Health Service. Relative rates of use of the two services were found by asking respondents: 'This year, how many times have you been to the doctor?' and 'How many times have you gone out in church to be prayed for when you were ill?' (The interviews were conducted in August, so rates for the previous 8 months were investigated.) On average, mem-bers had visited the doctor twice and had been prayed for 2.3 times. A positive correlation was found between rate of attendance and number of times prayed for, while a slight negative correlation was found between the rate of attendance and number of visits to the doctor.

The close relationship between attendance and use of divine healing, while partly attributable to the cognitive support given to members by the sectarian community, is also a result of the more frequent opportunities the high attender has for going out for prayer, and his closer contact with the Pentecostal lay referral structure. The slight inverse relationship between attendance and use of the NHS suggests that belief in divine healing did conflict with belief in conventional medicine, at least for certain Pentecostalists in certain circumstances. Again it cannot be assumed that this is a simple causal relationship but there appears to be an interaction between attendance and lack of faith in scientific medicine. Other factors operating to reduce use of the NHS among high attenders may have included their relatively less frequent interaction with non-Pentecostal lay referral structures and, possibly, their reduced opportunity of visiting the doctor, as evening surgery may have clashed with Assembly meetings.

The Assembly of God, then, constitutes a plausibility structure, reinforcing its members' deviant medical beliefs which were initially learned through the sect's agencies of socialization. By way of being a religious minority, the Assembly of God is also a medical cognitive minority. Aspects of its organization as a sect, notably its mechanisms of socialization and the intense involvement required of members at the expense of 'worldly' contacts, function to maintain its deviant medical beliefs.

Lay Referral Systems

How far does the sectarian organization of the Assembly of God provide for referral of potential patients to the deviant practitioner?

Each Assembly member belongs to two populations, the Assembly of God and the 'world', each of which has its own healing service (divine healing or scientific medicine), and its own lay medical culture which is more or less congruent with that of its professional healers.

It might therefore be hypothesized that:

1. Each community has its own, separate lay referral system,[14] organizing the direction of help-seeking behaviour by referral towards its own practitioner.

2. Due to the sectarian characteristics of the Assembly's organization, the Pentecostal lay referral structure will be more cohesive and extended than the non-Pentecostal lay referral structure.

And therefore:

3. The utilization rate of divine healing services will be higher than that of conventional medical services.

Concerning the first hypothesis, prayer was found to be more often preceded by Pentecostal consultations than by non-Pentecostal consultations; and visits to the doctor were more often preceded by non-Pentecostal consultations than Pentecostal consultations. There is thus some evidence to support the hypothesis that each community has its own separate lay referral structure, though there is considerable overlap. Consultation with Pentecostal spouses, for example, was common before use of doctor *or* prayer; and among the single and widowed women Pentecostal friends sometimes fetched both doctor and pastor in emergencies. The Pentecostal lay referral system refers potential patients to both doctor *and* pastor – a consequence of the Pentecostal 'lay culture' which tolerates the use of conventional medicine along with prayer.

The non-Pentecostal referral route to the doctor is taken mainly by the single and widowed who ask neighbours and flat-mates to fetch the doctor. Such encounters provide the opportunity for advice-giving or the confirmation of decisions already taken, rather than advice-seeking. The Pentecostal route to the pastor is via consultation with spouses, with Pentecostal friends who send for the pastor or encourage going out for prayer, or through informal contacts with the pastor himself.

Some evidence lending support to the second hypothesis was described previously. The Assembly members' loose connections with non-Pentecostal networks – due to their recent immigration, lack of relatives, and disapproval of worldly pursuits – and the tight-knitness of the Assembly community, with the high rate of attendance expected of members, suggest that the lay referral structures will be similarly relatively loose-knit (non-Pentecostal) and cohesive (Pentecostal).

Eliot Freidson includes extensive interaction in the network in his idea of the 'cohesiveness' of the lay referral structure. The extensiveness of each of the lay referral structures, as measured by the numbers of lay consultations prior to utilization, was in agreement with the hypothesized greater cohesion of the Pentecostal network. This was particularly true of serious illnesses, where only 2 of the 11 cases presented to the doctor were preceded by one non-Pentecostal consultation, while 4 of the 7 cases taken for prayer were preceded by one or two Pentecostal consultations.

Discussions concerning illness were found to be more frequent with Pentecostalists than with non-Pentecostalists. In spite of the possibilities of interaction with non-Pentecostal neighbours and friends, only 13 non-Pentecostal lay consultations were reported compared with 20 Pentecostal lay consultations. The Pentecostal lay referral structure is therefore somewhat more cohesive and extended than its non-Pentecostal counterpart.

There is, however, not much difference in the utilization rates of orthodox medicine and divine healing. In the first 8 months of the year considered, the 20 Assembly members interviewed had consulted the doctor 40 times and been out for prayer 46 times. While this lack of difference is partly attributable to referrals to the doctor through the Pentecostal lay referral system, and partly to the lack of gross differences in structure between the two lay referral systems, it could be that the non-confirmation of this hypothesis results from the fact that utilization of the dominant, professionalized services in a society does not *require* an extended, cohesive structure of lay referrals. These officially sanctioned services may most effectively be used by self-referred clients. Orthodox medical behaviour may not require the support of a local plausibility structure, while unorthodox medical behaviour – whether manifested in under-utilization of official services, or utilization of unorthodox services – requires a cohesive lay referral structure.

As clients of the official medical services, Assembly members are self-referred, particularly in serious illnesses; or they consult with only one or two others, often just using them to fetch the doctor. Use of the NHS in serious illness is taken for granted by most Pentecostalists, as participants in the 'world'. But as clients of divine, healing services, Assembly members tend to be ushered towards the pastor through informal contacts with fellow Pentecostalists. Again, this is most noticeable in serious illnesses where there is commonly a time lag between utilization of medical and divine healing services, during which Pentecostal friends may visit and recommend fetching the pastor. The Assembly's organization of its members towards divine healing illustrates the need for community support for the deviant illness behaviour resulting from deviant medical beliefs. It affords evidence of the low credibility of unorthodox beliefs when faced with the dominant medical belief system, in that their implementation requires extensive lay referrals even to attain a rate of utilization comparable with that of the NHS.

To summarize, two lay referral structures could be distinguished, the sect's and the 'world's', leading to utilization of the two healing services. While the sect's was rather more cohesive and extended than the world's, it did not result in a higher rate of utilization of divine healing than of conventional medical services, but rather it appeared to be necessary for the maintenance of deviant illness behaviour.[15]

Conclusion

While scientific and religious beliefs about the causation and treatment of illness may appear to be incompatible in many respects, it was found that members of the Assembly of God were able to hold both sets of beliefs simultaneously, without any conflict in practice. It was possible for divine healing to be used in conjunction with the physical methods of conventional medicine and for members to combine the use of both services, which they did particularly in the case of serious illness.

Assembly members did not often report experiencing a dilemma in deciding which medical service to choose. It was mainly when a member who was highly committed to belief in divine healing was faced with a fairly serious illness or a worsening chronic condition, that a dilemma was experienced. Among less committed members, or for more serious illnesses, use of the NHS was more readily accepted. Since the Assembly of God does not prohibit use of orthodox medical services, in serious illnesses members were not faced with the choice between breaking their religious principles by fetching the doctor, and refusing medical treatment altogether. The extent to which an unorthodox medical system conflicts with the orthodox one, and presents its adherents with an either/ or choice, depends partly on whether its treatment methods are physical or mental/spiritual. It is often a practical impossibility for systems of physical treatment such as naturopathy and homeopathy to be used in conjunction with allopathic medicine, so their utilization entails non-utilization of conventional medical services. Mental or spiritual methods of treatment, however, may conflict in principle with scientific medicine, but in practice they may be used together. Clients of hypnotherapists, Christian Science healers, faith healers, spiritualists, mesmerists, etc. may thus be able to avoid the dilemma of an either/or choice. It would be expected that the greater the conflict between an unorthodox medical system and the establishment, both in theory and practice, the stronger the social structural supports needed to maintain the plausibility of the deviant knowledge, and the more cohesive and extended the lay referral structure required to maintain a given rate of utilization. Since the conflict would be expected to be most acute in deviant physical medical systems, these would be expected to require the strongest social structural supports for the utilization of their services. Mental and spiritual systems, if used in place of conventional medical services, would be expected to require equally strong social structural supports. But if the conflict is avoided by utilizing both services, then a viable rate of utilization of the deviant service may be achieved with a less extended and less cohesive lay referral structure. However, as with the Assembly of God, even where the deviant system is primarily used to supplement the dominant one, as a belief system held by a minority group its credibility is still threatened by dominant medical beliefs, and utilization of its services still requires a fairly cohesive and extensive lay referral structure.

The Pentecostal lay referral structure was found to organize potential patients towards utilization of divine healing, but not to direct them away from the NHS. Where an unorthodox medical system is used as an alternative to scientific medicine, it would be expected that the medical cognitive minority would have to exercise some form of social control to prevent use of the NHS, in addition to referring patients towards the deviant practitioner. It seems likely that only in the most sectarian religious groups is such a condition approached. Refusal of medical treatment in life-endangering illness appears to be a rare phenomenon peculiar to strict sects – such as Christian Science and Jehovah's Witnesses – and not found among the more denominationalized religious groups such as the Assemblies of God.

The clientele of unorthodox systems based on physical treatment, use of which entails non-use of conventional medicine, are not organized into groups, in Britain at least, with agencies of social control and sufficiently cohesive and extended lay referral structures to ensure the exclusive use of the deviant service. Such medical services therefore tend to be used as a last resort in serious illness, not as an alternative system.

Science and religion, both of which have developed knowledge about disease treatment, provide answers which in some ways complement and in some ways conflict with one another. The differentiation of knowledge within the scientific and religious traditions has resulted in a diversity of treatment systems, of which the allopathic scientific system is dominant in Britain. The minority systems, varying in the degree to which their implementation conflicts with the dominant medical system, also vary in the degree to which their social organization enables them actually to utilize their deviant medical practitioners. It seems likely that only in the sectarian organization of minority religious groups are the structural supports of the deviant medical system strong enough to ensure the perpetuation and implementation of its unorthodox medical beliefs.

NOTES AND REFERENCES

1 Peter Berger, *The Social Reality of Religion,* Faber & Faber, London, 1967.

2 *Assemblies of God Yearbook 1968-1969.*

3 John Highet, 'Scottish religious adherence', *British Journal of Sociology,* Vol. 4, 1953, pp. 142-159.

4 In *Assemblies of God Yearbook 1968-1969,* op. cit.

5 For the notion of conversionist sect, see Bryan R. Wilson, 'An analysis of sect development', *American Sociological Review,* Vol. 24, No. 1, 1959, pp. 3-15.

6 These theories have a quasi-karmic character. For a non-Christian parallel, see Roy Wallis, 'The Aetherius Society: a case study in the formation of a mystagogic congregation', *Sociological Review,* Vol. 22, No. 1, 1974, pp. 27-44, reprinted in Roy Wallis (ed.), *Sectarianism: Analyses of Religious and Non-Religious Sects,* Peter Owen, London, 1975.

7 Max Weber, *The Sociology of Religion,* Methuen, London, 1966, pp. 138-150.

8 Ibid., pp. 142-143.

9 2 Tim. 3:12, quoted in the Assembly periodical *Redemption Tidings,* 23 July, 1970.

10 *Divine Healing and Co-operation between Doctors and Clergy,* Report of the BMA Committee,British Medical Association, London, 1955.

11 As David Mechanic's findings would lead one to expect; David Mechanic, 'The concept of illness behaviour', *Journal of Chronic Diseases,* Vol. 15, 1962, pp. 189-194.

12 Roland Robertson, *The Sociological Interpretation of Religion,* Blackwell, Oxford, 1970.

13 Registrar General, *Census 1961 Scotland,* (Internal migration, National and local summary tables), Her· Majesty's Stationery Office, London, 1964.

14 For discussion of the lay referral system, see Eliot Freidson, *Profession of Medicine,* Dodd, Mead and Co., New York, 1970.

15 See also Gillian Allen (née Branch) *Pentecostalism as a Deviant Medical System,* Unpub. M.Litt. thesis, University of Aberdeen, 1970. Mrs Allen gratefully acknowledges the advice of Gordon Horobin, Director of the MRC Medical Sociology Unit, Aberdeen.

PART THREE:

UTILIZATION OF ORTHODOX AND
UNORTHODOX MEDICINE

Julian Roebuck and Robert Quan

7

Health-Care Practices in the American Deep South

Introduction

Traditionally, part of the subject matter of ethnographers has been the study of native theories of illness and healing practices.[1] Moreover, a growing interest in the field of culture and medical care has led to intensive work on the nature and meaning of folk medicine.[2] More recently, some sociologists have become interested in the subject matter of deviant, non-Western, medical theories and practices within the United States.[3] The question has been raised as to whether or not these competing systems actually satisfy patient needs supposedly fulfilled by scientifically legitimated health-care practices.[4] The practices include: the use of over-the-counter nostrums[5] for self-diagnosed maladies; the use of spurious treatment devices and treatments; and the use of marginal, illegal and unorthodox healers. The present sociological trend in the United States is to study these alternative avenues to health care within the framework of deviant behaviour.[6] There is a need for several field-work studies throughout the United States in order to determine what groups of people choose what kinds of health-care practices. More specifically, we need studies on various population groups to determine what segments of the population utilize what kinds of spurious health-care practices. In this paper a lower-class sample from Mississippi is analysed.

The study focuses on a deep Southern rural area that has similar characteristics to some underdeveloped countries which still adhere to folk beliefs and non-Western practices in the area of health care. The town in which the research was conducted and

141

the county in which it is located afford a substantial population base of lower-class blacks and whites. It was assumed that health-care orientations and practices geared towards self-care and folk medicine would prevail here more than in cosmopolitan settings.

The primary purpose of the study was to determine the comparative health-care practices obtaining among lower-class blacks and lower-class whites from a small Mississippi town of approximately 11,000 population (a rural area service centre). We examined the behaviour of these two groups when seeking medical attention for illness and/or self-diagnosis and treatment of medical problems encountered over a period of one year. In this comparison, we attempted to ascertain the medical and treatment orientations of the sample, i.e. how the respondents defined illness and what action they resorted to as a consequence of illness. Special emphasis was placed on deviant health-care practices.

The interview instrument was derived from a review of the literature and from Roebuck and Hunter's typology of deviant health-care practices, i.e. (1) health practitioners; (2) spurious nostrums; (3) spurious treatment devices; and (4) spurious treatments.[7] In seeking to explain why respondents resort to certain health-care practices we employed a modified version of Berkanovic and Reeder's [8] three determinant models for health-care services: (1) unequal access based on deficient income as related to inequalities of health-care utilization; (2) a culture of poverty, based on low educational levels, that renders poor people unable to make effective use of most health-care systems; (3) cultural and social psychological attributes related to ethnicity and social economic status.

We included variables found in all three of Berkanovic and Reeder's models except for a few social psychological variables; and we included age and residence, excluded by them. Unlike Berkanovic and Reeder, our study was also not confined only to health-care practices utilized through the services of M.Ds. After determining the health-care practices among our two separate samples (blacks and whites), we examined the differences in health-care practices with regard to age, income, and education in both samples.

Our typology classified spurious healers into three major practitioner groups: (1) consensus healers; (2) marginal healers; (3) illegal healers. Additionally, the categories of nostrums, treatment devices, and treatments were expanded to obtain a wider response in the area of spurious health-care practices.

We arrived at the following schema in the review of the literature: (1) self-diagnosis and treatment practices as related to the purveyance of fraudulent or misrepresented nostrums; (2) practices related to the purveyance of fraudulent, non-functionable, or misrepresented treatment devices and treatments; (3) practices related to the use of illegal, marginal, and/or unorthodox healers.

Self-diagnosis, Treatment, and Nostrums

Self-diagnosis and self-treatment of all kinds of health problems seem to be a great American tradition.[9] Kenneth L. Jones, *et al.,* in their book *Consumer Health*, posit some reasons for this widespread practice:

As the country was being settled, doctors were very few and transportation was very poor, so self-treatment was a necessity. Even today, most physicians are very busy, appointments are difficult to get, and for many people, the cost of proper medical care is discouraging. For many residents of rural areas and ethnic ghetto areas of large cities, transportation to medical facilities remains a problem. In addition to these factors, there is the continuing barrage of advertisements for self-treatment products for ailments of every description.[10]

Certainly, many Americans throughout the social structure resort to self-diagnosis, treatment, and spurious nostrums. Some dangers involved in attempting self-diagnosis and treatment of any kind of symptom are: (1) that a major disorder may easily be misdiagnosed as some common or simple problem and treated as such without ever investigating its significance; (2) such practice delays a person from seeking adequate professional medical attention; (3) not all over-the-counter preparations are safe to take, i.e. some are dangerous when used in excessive amounts in the presence of certain physical disorders, or in combination with other medicines. Sometimes self-medicators are oblivious to certain critical signs of illness such as severe, prolonged, and unusual symptoms which call for attention. Furthermore, a national health-care study disclosed: 'A considerable portion of the American public disregards the common warning on non-prescriptive medicine labels to see a physician if symptoms persist more than a few days.'[11]

For the purposes of this study, most nostrums[12] may be classified under two major headings: super-health nostrums, and super-corrective health nostrums. The first category consists of nostrums whose expected benefits are oriented towards vitality. Among this group are multiple vitamins, vitamins, and tonics. The vitality theme runs rampant in the promotion of nutritional supplements and in the convincing pronouncements of 'health food advocates' who recommend vitamins as a panacea for tiredness and lack of energy due to faulty diets. Furthermore, the belief that taking vitamins will provide almost anyone with more 'pep' and energy is the most common widespread misconception based upon questionable conventional wisdom.[13]

The second category, super-corrective health nostrums, consists of nostrums whose expected benefits are oriented towards restoration of health. These nostrums consist of weight-reduction products, bowel-movement aids, indigestion aids, smoking-deterrent aids, haemorrhoid remedies, and mouthwashes. Many who use these products do not distinguish in their thinking between a cure and symptomatic relief. The distinction between reducing discomfort and eliminating the underlying cause of discomfort is not sufficiently understood, it has been argued in a national study on health-care practices and opinions.[14]

Treatment Devices and Treatments

Many Americans utilize a plethora of treatment devices and treatments that are not prescribed by M.Ds. Arthritis and rheumatism comprise a number of diseases attended to by health quacks who prescribe and/or utilize an assortment of treatment devices and treatments for these diseases. Pain and discomfort in this area are frequently not assuaged by M.Ds. The following spurious and worthless treatment devices and treatments are typically employed: vibrators, heat pads, infra-red lamps, copper bracelets, zinc discs, health spas, uranium tunnels, and radio-active ore treatments.[15]

Unorthodox Medical Practices by Marginal and Illegal Healers

Practitioners in this category follow a system of medical and scientific thought that is unacceptable to the scientific and medical establishment. Healers such as chiropractors and osteopaths, although licensed to practice in most states of America, are still considered marginal.[16] Chiropractors and most osteopaths are defined as quacks by many M.Ds. Illegal healers such as folk practitioners, spiritualists and sorcerers operate without a licence to practise in the United States. One distinction to be made between medical doctors and illegal healers rests upon the medical orientations of the two. Scientific medical orientations to illness may be termed allopathic, i.e. treating illness as arising from disease entities within the body (germs). Conversely, the medical orientations of illegal healers are based upon organic, spiritual, or metaphysical causes.[17] Moreover, the treatment used by illegal healers is purportedly directed towards eliminating the cause of the problem, rather than just the symptoms as (the illegal healer claims) is the case with allopathic medicine.

Summary

Thus it can be seen that there exists a plethora of spurious nostrums, treatment devices, treatments, and health practitioners, widely advertised and used by the American public. In spite of the fact that our modern society has a highly scientific technology and a literate population, the norms guiding health care throughout the social structure are yet unclear. The literature clearly indicates that the medical and scientific establishments have failed to promulgate or disseminate a uniform set of health-care norms acceptable to large numbers of people throughout the social structure.

Therefore, a conflict of norms governing health-care practices exists between those subscribing to scientific medicine (practitioners and patients) and those advocating and utilizing deviant health-care practices. Further confusion on the part of Americans in regard to what constitutes 'good health', as well as what to do about 'bad health', complicates the matter considerably.[18]

Methodology and Description of Sample

We sought to test the hypothesis that ethnic variation (considered as a cultural variable) determines variation in health-care practices, since an idea prevails throughout the United States that there is a black culture which is radically distinct from a white culture. First we tested for differences in health-care practices between blacks and whites. Next we controlled for age (a measure of cultural immersion), since we reasoned that given the rapidly changing technological nature of medicine over the last few decades, old people would be more likely to lag behind modern health-care practices than younger persons. Then we controlled for income since this is one measure of unequal access to health services. The tests we imposed on the data sought to differentiate an 'access' explanation and a 'cultural' explanation of differences in health-care practices. If income alone could predict source of health-care practices, there would be evidence in favour of an access explanation. Finally, we controlled for education (which we took as one measure of the culture of poverty) since it is thought those people in the lower class with the least amount of education are the most 'entrenched' in the culture of poverty. If education could predict the source of health-care practices, the culture-of-poverty thesis would be supported. The poor, by implication, need to learn the skills essential to use the system in seeking adequate health care.[19]

The sample consisted of 100 households: 50 blacks and 50 whites drawn from the lower-class residential areas. These areas were selected on the advice of six authoritative local informants.[20] Households were then sampled within these areas.[21] In all of the

100 occupied dwellings selected, a member of the household over 21 years of age (residing full-time at the given address) consented to be interviewed, except for three subjects in the white sample who refused to participate. Three new households were drawn from each of their respective areas for replacement. A pretested, structured, fixed alternative, interview schedule was employed, which also provided for open-ended responses in the area of self-diagnosis and treatment, and respondents' definitions of illness.

Our sample showed an over-representation of females (75 per cent) to males (25 per cent). The age of our sample ranged from 20 to 86 years. Blacks were generally younger than whites. The most frequent religious preference was Southern Baptist, accounting for 78 per cent of the total sample. Respondents' average educational level was about fifth to sixth grade. The majority of our sample (68 per cent) held jobs at the semi-skilled and unskilled levels. None of the respondents were working at or above managerial level. Fifty-six per cent of blacks and 62 per cent of whites were housewives. Fifteen per cent were unemployed at the time of the interview. Solid rural backgrounds were predominant (57 per cent). Household membership showed black families with more adult members than whites, and also more children. The majority of our sample (57 per cent) were married. The annual gross income (self-reported) for whites ranged from $600-$8,500 with a median of $1,800. Black income ranged from $500-$5,000 with a median of $1,200. Most respondents' incomes were supplemented to a large extent by public assistance or welfare payments.

For the purpose of our analysis, the first dependent variable, *health practitioners*, was trichotomized into: (a) *consensus healer* [22] – medical doctor; (b) *marginal healers* – chiropractor, osteopath, pharmacist, podiatrist, nurse-midwife; (c) *illegal healers* – folk practitioner, spiritualist, sorcerer.

The second dependent variable, *nostrums*, was dichotomized into: (a) *super-health nostrums* – this category included various tonics, vitamin and multiple vitamin preparations; (b) *super-corrective health nostrums* – this category included various laxative, digestive and haemorrhoid treatments, slimming pills, mouthwashes, etc.

For the purposes of our analysis, we classified nostrum users into three categories: (1) *user* – three or more super-health and/or super-corrective nostrums; (2) *mixer* – one or two super-health and/or super-corrective nostrums; (3) *non-user* – doesn't use any nostrums.

The third dependent variable, *treatment devices*, was represented by the following items: vibrators, heat pads, infra-red lamps, copper bracelets and zinc discs. For purposes of analysis we divided respondents into users and non-users of devices.

The independent variable was *ethnicity:* black and white. If ethnicity alone could predict the source of health-care practice, then the cultural explanation would be supported, i.e. a black culture explanation. To determine if any effects were made by age, income and education on health-care practices between lower-class whites and lower-class blacks, we controlled for each of these variables.[23]

Quantitative Findings

Health-Care Practitioners

Table 1 presents type of practitioner utilized by ethnicity and shows statistically significant differences between blacks and whites. White respondents utilized legitimate healers more frequently than black respondents. This variation may be based on the whites' higher social status, greater integration into society, and a consequent adherence to Western scientific medicine.

TABLE 1:   TYPE OF PRACTITIONER USED BY ETHNIC GROUP[24]

	Black	White
Consensus Healer only	48%	68%
Combination M.D. and Others	42%	24%
Marginal Healers	4%	8%
Illegal Healers	6%	0%
(N)	(50)	(50)
Tau C = .20		**P < .01

Table 2 presents type of practitioner utilized by ethnicity while controlling for age (a measure of cultural immersion). The results revealed statistically significant relationships only in the old age group. Old age whites utilized the medical doctor more frequently than did old age blacks. Old age blacks also more frequently employed a combination of M.D. and other healers than did old age whites. Blacks in the old age group more frequently utilized illegal healers than did whites. Again these findings indicate blacks are less oriented towards scientific medicine than whites.

TABLE 2: TYPE OF PRACTITIONER USED BY AGE AND ETHNIC GROUP

	Young Age[25]		Middle Age		Old Age	
	Black	*White*	*Black*	*White*	*Black*	*White*
Consensus Healer	60%	50%	47.6%	60%	42.1%	73.5%
Combination M.D. and Others	30%	50%	52.4%	20%	36.8%	20.6%
Marginal Healers	0%	0%	0%	20%	10.5%	5.9%
Illegal Healers	10%	0%	0%	0%	10.5%	0%
(N)	(10)	(6)	(21)	(10)	(19)	(34)
	Tau C = − .02		Tau C = .02		Tau C = .32	
	$P \neq .05$		$P \neq .05$		$**P < .01$	

Table 3 presents type of practitioner used by income and ethnicity. When controlling for income, an access measure, we found a statistically significant relationship between ethnicity and practitioner utilization only for the low income group. Within this low income group, the utilization of the M.D. was highest for whites. Low income blacks utilized the combination of M.D. and other healers more than low income whites. Though low income blacks utilized marginal healers less than whites, they were the exclusive users of illegal healers. Again this indicates the differential in the two groups' orientations to scientific medicine.

TABLE 3: TYPE OF PRACTITIONER USED BY INCOME AND ETHNIC GROUP

	Low Income		High Income	
	Black	*White*	*Black*	*White*
Consensus Healer	44.1%	76.5%	56.3%	46.7%
Combination M.D. and Others	44.1%	17.6%	37.5%	40%
Marginal Healers	2.9%	5.9%	6.3%	13.3%
Illegal Healers	8.8%	0%	0%	0%
(N)	(34)	(34)	(16)	(15)
	Tau C = .32		Tau C = − .12	
	$**P < .01$		$P \neq .05$	

Table 4 presents type of practitioner used by ethnicity when controlling for education, a measure of the culture of poverty.[26] We found a statistically significant relationship for low education only. Low educated whites represented the largest percentage of M.D. use (80 per cent). Low educated blacks utilized the combination of M.D. and other healers more than their white counterparts indicating a mixture of scientific medicine with deviant health-care practices. Furthermore, low educated blacks were the only users of illegal healers. This latter finding indicates that blacks think there are some maladies beyond the treatment province of M.Ds. On the other hand, low educated whites used marginal healers more frequently than low educated blacks. Perhaps whites are more cognizant of marginal healers than are blacks, though they eschew illegal healers. When controlling for education, the relationship between practitioner utilization and ethnicity disappeared for the high income group.

TABLE 4: TYPE OF PRACTITIONER USED BY EDUCATION AND ETHNIC GROUP

	Low Education		High Education	
	Black	*White*	*Black*	*White*
Consensus Healer	40.6%	80%	61.1%	56%
Combination M.D. and Others	46.9%	12%	33.3%	36%
Marginal Healers	3.1%	8%	5.6%	8%
Illegal Healers	9.4%	0%	0%	0%
(N)	(32)	(25)	(10)	(6)
	Tau C = .37		Tau C = − .05	
	**P < .01		P ≠ .05	

Health-Care Nostrums

We first tested the relationship of nostrum utilization by ethnicity, and found no significant differences. A further test was made by controlling for age. Table 5 reveals a statistically significant positive relationship between ethnicity and nostrum utilization in the middle age group, i.e. middle age whites tend to be users while middle age blacks tend to be mixers. Additionally, a significant negative relationship was found in the young age group, i.e. young whites tend to be mixers while young blacks tend to be mixers and users. Examining trends across age categories, it is seen th t nostrum use decreased among whites with increasing age. The tendency for blacks to use nostrums decreased with age at the user level, but increased at the mixer level. The increase of mixers in the old age category seems to indicate that although respondents' frequency of use is not as high as that of users, they still use nostrums (but with a lower frequency at old age than in their younger days). Moreover, old age whites (11.8 per cent) were non-users which shows that they rely on nostrums less than blacks in the same age category.

TABLE 5: TYPE OF USER OF HEALTH-CARE NOSTRUMS BY AGE

	Young Age		Middle Age		Old Age	
	Black	*White*	*Black*	*White*	*Black*	*White*
User	50%	16.7%	47.6%	70%	36.8%	32.4%
Mixer	50%	83.3%	52.4%	30%	63.2%	55.9%
Non-User	0%	0%	0%	0%	0%	11.8%
(N)	(10)	(6)	(21)	(10)	(19)	(34)
	Tau B $= -.33$		Tau B $= .21$		Tau C $= -.11$	
	$P < .05$		$P < .05$		$P \neq .05$	

No significant relationship between ethnicity and nostrum use was found when income was controlled. However, high income blacks and whites were found to use nostrums more frequently than the low income groups. More mixers were found among low income blacks than among high income blacks. Perhaps this later finding indicates that low income, old age blacks use nostrums less frequently now than they did when they were younger (and were more financially able to purchase them). No blacks were reported to be non-users; however, there were a few white non-users in both income categories.

Table 6 presents type of nostrum user by ethnicity and education. No significant relationship for high education was found. However, for low education, the findings indicate a statistically significant negative relationship between ethnicity and nostrum use, i.e. among the less educated respondents, all blacks fell into the user and mixer categories, while most whites were mixers. Some whites were users but (unlike blacks) some were non-users. The high educated black and white categories contained more mixers. There were no black non-users, while white non-users decreased with an increased education.

TABLE 6: TYPE OF USER OF HEALTH-CARE NOSTRUMS BY EDUCATION AND ETHNIC GROUP

| | Low Education | | High Education | |
	Black	White	Black	White
User	40.6%	24%	50%	52%
Mixer	59.4%	64%	50%	44%
Non-User	0%	12%	0%	4%
(N)	(32)	(25)	(18)	(25)
	Tau C = − .23		Tau C = .00	
	**P < .01		P ≠ .05	

Health-Care Treatment Devices

The third area of health-care practices tested was utilization of devices. No statistically significant relationship was found between utilization of treatment devices and ethnicity; however blacks reported more frequent use of devices than did whites. To determine if age affected the relationship between ethnicity and device use, we controlled for it. Although no statistically significant results were found, the use of devices is generally lowest for young blacks and whites, highest for the middle age group, and tapers down for the old age group. Perhaps the middle age group is in a better financial position to afford these devices.

Next we controlled for income and found no statistically significant differences. However, the data indicated that high income whites reported the greatest percentage of device use. Reasoning that education might affect the relationship between ethnicity and device use, we controlled for it, but the analysis again yielded no statistically significant results.

SUMMARY: QUANTITATIVE FINDINGS

Practitioner utilization varied significantly by ethnicity. When controlling for age this relationship disappeared for young and middle age groups and became stronger for old age groups. We suggest that the young and middle age groups are becoming more acculturated to modern health-care practices. Additionally, younger blacks are using legitimate health-care practices more frequently than older blacks. Old blacks tend to rely on spurious healers in combination with M.Ds. Controlling for income, the relationship between ethnicity and type of practitioner used disappeared for the high income group, but became stronger for the low income group, i.e. whites still used the M.D. more than did blacks. Blacks used illegitimate practitioners more often than did whites. Whites more frequently used established healers and marginal healers. In the high income black and white groups the relationships between practitioner use and ethnicity remained unchanged. Controlling for education, the relationship remained significant for the low education group only, i.e. low educated whites used the M.D. more than their black counterparts who used a combination of M.D. and other healers.

The relationship between nostrum use and ethnicity was not found to be statistically significant. A positive relationship was found for the middle age group when controlling for age, i.e. middle age whites were users while middle age blacks were users and mixers. Additionally, when controlling for education an inverse relationship was found for low educated respondents, i.e. all blacks fell into the user and mixer categories while most whites were primarily mixers.

In the area of device utilization, the relationship between ethnicity and device use remained the same despite controls placed on age, income, and education. Respondents indicated no use of health-care treatments such as 'uranium tunnels', 'radioactive ore' or 'health spas'. Since our respondents were all lower class, these findings regarding device and treatment use may reflect lack of access (availability and money for) and knowledge of treatment devices and treatments *vis-à-vis* nostrum use.

QUALITATIVE FINDINGS: WHITE SAMPLE

Open-ended Questions

> Question II.F: How sick do you and the above person(s) [i.e.
> other members of the household] get before you
> seek treatment?

An overwhelming number of whites (44 per cent) stated that they sought treatment following 'prolonged illness' or 'a high fever'. Twenty per cent stated they sought treatment after noting 'any sign of illness', 'discomfort', or 'not feeling right'. Twenty per cent claimed they went for treatment when 'I fall out' (i.e. collapse), or when 'I'm so sick that I need to be carried to the doctor'. Sixteen per cent reported they sought treatment only if they 'had to quit work' or 'can't work'. A clear majority of white respondents (64 per cent) stated that they solicited medical attention before illness got so serious that they had to quit work or be hospitalized. This delaying practice is not in keeping with physicians' warnings to seek treatment if symptoms persist for more than a few days.

> Question III.G: Why, or under what conditions would you go
> to the above mentioned practitioners?

The majority of white respondents (52 per cent) stated that they would not utilize any healer, but an M.D. This finding substantiates to some degree the quantitative findings regarding M.D. utilization. However, 10 per cent reported they would see other healers provided a physician recommended it. Only 4 per cent said they would see a healer other than the M.D. as a last resort, i.e. if the M.D. could not help them. A substantial number of respondents (34 per cent) reported the effectiveness of the chiropractor for back trouble and the spiritualist for prayers. The chiropractor was the most frequently used marginal healer. This substantiates our quantitative findings about chiropractors. The acceptance of the spiritualist as a contingent healer probably reflects the respondents' strong fundamentalist religious backgrounds.

Unsolicited Comments

The unsolicited comments proffered by the respondents were at times more revealing than those questions handled quantitatively. Space permits only a few examples here.[27] These comments served as a check on our quantitative findings, and also added additional information. In the main they confirmed both the quantitative and open-ended disclosures. Beyond this they told us in many different ways that:

1   Although they go to M.Ds. they state a lack of faith in them, e.g. 'Well I don't like to go to the doctor anyway, but where else am I going to go? They think they know too much, and they don't like to tell you anything or give you the time of day.'

2   Furthermore, this lack of faith is reinforced by the prescription medication which they impatiently feel 'does no good,' e.g. 'Those pills made me dizzy and sleepy, so I quit taking them; they didn't do no good.'

3   Additionally, they exhibit little knowledge of the divergent roles of health practitioners, e.g. 'The druggist knows what doctors know about medicines, chiropractors know something too, after all, they're doctors too.'

4   Finally, they exhibit an independence of belief and behaviour in health-care practices, e.g. 'I hardly ever get sick, but when I do, I just go downtown to the drug store'; or (about chiropractors) 'A friend said it's cheaper to go see him instead of a doctor. I don't like to go to either one if I can help it.'

QUANTITATIVE FINDINGS: BLACK SAMPLE

Open-ended Questions

Question II.F: How sick do you and the above person(s) [i.e. other members of the household] get before you seek treatment?

Only 4 per cent of the black sample stated they sought treatment following 'any sign of sickness' or 'hurt'. Thirty-two per cent reported that they sought treatment only after 'prolonged illness' accompanying a fever or the flu, or 'spells' derived from high blood pressure. A surprising number of blacks (48 per cent) claimed they sought treatment only when forced to 'quit work'. A typical quote in this direction was: 'Quitting work means losing money, and I can't afford to do that.' A smaller percentage of black respondents (14 per cent) revealed that they sought treatment only after they 'fell out', literally meaning a collapse.

> Question III.G: Why, or under what conditions would you go to the above mentioned practitioners?

Twenty-four per cent of the black respondents chose to see the M.D., eschewing other healers. Only 6 per cent reported they would see other healers provided the M.D. advised them to do so. Twelve per cent of the black sample claimed they would see other healers only if it were the last resort. Typical responses in this category, revealing respondents' scepticism of M.Ds., were: 'The doctor just gives me drugs and doesn't make my back feel any better' (arthritis sufferer), or 'I would try a chiropractor for back trouble if I got no results from an M.D.' Blacks generally thought deviant healers, i.e. healers other than M.Ds., were effective. Fifty per cent claimed such support, e.g. 'All [healers] are effective in their field,' or 'Yes, I would try a spiritualist for heart trouble or to help cure a disease.' Eight per cent reported they did not like doctors or any healers at all.

Unsolicited Comments

The unsolicited comments substantiated the quantitative findings and open-ended questions. More importantly, the respondents' comments amplified their health-care orientations in the following ways:

1   The cost of hiring a midwife for childbirth costs much less than

having a child at the hospital. For example, 'My child [delivery] only cost me $50 and she [midwife] even takes care of me and tells me what drugs to buy at the store.'

2   They reveal a scepticism of Western orthodox medicine and hold firm beliefs rooted in magic and superstition. For example, 'I saw Sister Cherokee [spiritualist] and she rubbed some olive oil on the back of my neck and told me I was suffering from high blood – exactly what the doctor told me !'

3   They dislike surgery or 'going under the knife' and would seek other alternatives if possible. For example, 'The last thing I'd do is to have some doctor cutting away on me.'

4   Some blacks believe the hoodoo man [sorcerer] can lift spells from them, e.g. 'The doctor thought I had a stroke because I couldn't move, but the hoodoo man said someone had placed stumbling blocks in front of me and he chased it away.'

CONCLUSION

The qualitative analysis of both samples substantiated the quantitative findings which showed a difference in health-care practices between the two samples. Both samples revealed similarities in their orientations to the M.D. Whites were predominant users of M.Ds. over blacks, yet both samples were sceptical about the M.Ds.' effectiveness in contrast to other healers, especially the chiropractor. In this regard, blacks utilized the M.D. in combination with other healers, i.e. marginal and illegal healers. Blacks were predominant in the utilization of illegal healers. Both samples exhibited little knowledge of health practitioners in general. The health-care orientations of both samples disclosed in the qualitative findings showed that neither whites nor blacks were strongly oriented towards scientific medicine. Whites verbalized less scepticism about scientific medicine than blacks. Furthermore, as nostrum and device users, these two samples exhibited an independence of belief and behaviour in health care, i.e. a firm reliance in themselves while performing self-diagnosis and self-treatment for illness. The qualitative differences found between both samples as determined by a content analysis of the open-ended questions and the additional unsolicited comments revealed the following general distinctions:

1 Blacks revealed a higher threshold of sickness before seeking treatment for illness *vis-à-vis* whites.

2 Blacks were less oriented to Western scientific medicine than were whites. This fact is demonstrated in their use of illegal healers and less reliance on M.Ds.

3 Blacks reported less faith in M.Ds. than did whites.

4 Blacks believed in the effectiveness of the sorcerer as an effective metaphysician. Whites neither utilized the sorcerer nor did they verbalize any comments in this direction.

5 Many lower-class black females utilized the unlicensed midwife (although licensed nurse-midwives are available to them) whereas all whites utilized a hospital for childbirth.

NOTES AND REFERENCES

1 Rene Dubois, *Man, Medicine, and Environment,* The New American Library, New York, 1961; Oscar Lewis, *Life in a Mexican Village: Tepoztlan Restudied,* The University of Illinois Press, Urbana, Illinois, 1951; and George M. Foster, *Problems in Intercultural Health Programs,* Social Science Research Council Pamphlet, No. 12, New York, 1959.

2 Thomas McCorkle, 'Chiropractic: a deviant theory and treatment in contemporary western culture', *Human Organization,* Vol. 20, Spring 1961, pp. 20-23.

3 Julian B. Roebuck and Robert B. Hunter, 'The awareness of health-care quackery as deviant behaviour', *Journal of Health and Social Behaviour,* Vol. 13, June 1972, pp. 162-166.

4 Legitimate health-care practices are those that are sanctioned by the scientific and medical establishments, particularly the American Medical Association.

5 A nostrum is a patent medicine. The American Medical Association (AMA) finds nostrums (a majority of which are called OTCs, over-the-counter medicines) to be ineffective.

6 Julian B. Roebuck and Robert B. Hunter, 'Medical quackery as deviant behavior', *Criminology*, Vol. 8, May 1970, pp. 46-62.

7 Ibid.

8 Emil Berkanovic and Leo G. Reeder, 'Ethnic, economic and social psychological factors in the source of medical care', *Social Problems*, Vol. 21, No. 1, Fall 1973, pp. 246-259.

9 Self-reliant people generally think they understand their own health better than most doctors. In fact, despite their orientation to doctors as being: 'I always try to do exactly what the doctor advises, even if it is not very pleasant or easy', when given a medicine that proves to be ineffective, they usually resort to their own knowledge, indicating a conflict between normative attitudes and self-prescribed behaviour. See Karen Dunnell and Ann Cartwright, *Medicine Takers, Prescribers and Hoarders*, Routledge & Kegan Paul, Boston,1972, pp. 57-58.

10 Kenneth L. Jones, *et al.*, *Consumer Health*, Cranfield Press, San Francisco, 1971, pp. 29-30. Also with the increasing popularity of acupuncture therapy, it is possible to obtain home-study supplies and information for learning this art through the mail.

11 National Technical Information Service, U.S. Department of Commerce, *A Study of Health Practice and Opinion*, U.S. Department of Commerce, Springfield, Virginia, 1972, pp. 30-31.

12 For discussions on health myths that have been promulgated and utilized by vested economic interests to promote sale of their products see: M. Daniel Tatkon, *The Great Vitamin Hoax*, Macmillan, New York, 1968; James Cook, *Remedies and Rackets*, Norton, New York, 1958; Ralph L. Smith, *Health Hucksters*, Crowell, New York, 1968; Stewart H. Holbrook, *The Golden Age of Quackery*, Macmillan, New York, 1959.

13 M. Daniel Tatkon, *The Great Vitamin Hoax*, op. cit.

14 National Technical Information Service, U.S. Department of Commerce, op. cit., pp. 63-64.

15 For discussions on spurious treatment devices and treatments, see American Medical Association pamphlet, 'Health quackery: arthritis', AMA, Chicago, Illinois, 1968; James L. Goddard, 'Drug and deviance quackery', in AMA Proceedings, *Third National Congress on Medical Quackery*, Chicago, Illinois, October 1966, pp. 7-14; R. Walred, *The Misrepresentation of Arthritis Drugs and Devices in the United States*, The Arthritis and Rheumatism Foundation, New York, 1960.

16 For a discussion of chiropractors, see Walter I. Wardwell, 'A marginal professional role: the chiropractor', in E. Gartly Jaco (ed.), *Patients, Physicians, and Illness*, Free Press, Glencoe, Illinois, 1958, pp. 421-433. See also his paper in the present volume. For an excellent account of a chiropractic clinic, see James B. Cowie and Julian B. Roebuck, *An Ethnography*

of a Chiropractic Clinic: Definitions of a Deviant Situation, Free Press, New York, forthcoming.

17 See W. G. Cannon, 'Voodoo death', *American Anthropologist,* Vol. 44, No. 2, pp. 169-181.

18 The U.S. Department of Commerce in its national study, *A Study of Health Practices and Opinions,* carried out in 1972, report that many victims of health fallacies seem to be striving for 'super health'. They state, 'while physicians might define good health as simply the absence of bad health, many laymen see good health as a state *beyond* the mere absence of any disorder. Thus good health is not just normal health. Since it transcends the mere absence of disorder, it does not occur naturally, but must be deliberately worked at.' p. xviii. See also 'General Conclusions', pp. xi-xviii.

19 The interview schedule employed in this study may be obtained from Julian B. Roebuck, Professor of Sociology, Mississippi State University.

20 This 'jury opinion method' is discussed by William J. Goode and Paul K. Hatt, *Methods in Social Research,* McGraw-Hill, New York, 1952, pp. 237-238. The composition of the six-member jury was as follows: a white county agent, a white mayor, a white member of the city planning commission, a black social worker, a black medical doctor, and a black minister. All were town knowledgeables; and especially the last three members provided the researcher with entrée into the black community to allay any fears concerning the study.

21 A purposive proportionate cluster sample modified after Kish was employed. For an exploration of purposive sampling, see C. Seltiz, M. Jahoda, *et al., Research Methods in Social Relations,* Holt Rinehart and Winston, New York, 1959, pp. 520-521. For a discussion of cluster groupings, see Leslie Kish, *Survey Sampling,* John Wiley and Sons, New York, pp. 148-194. We are indebted to Professor Edna Ruth Davis, Head of the Social Work Department at Mississippi State University, for her assistance in the construction of our sampling techniques.

22 The consensus healer or medical doctor is the only sanctioned healer holding a mandate to practise by the American Medical Association, government agencies, the scientific community, commercial associations and state agencies.

23 Norman Nie, *et al., Statistical Package for the Social Sciences,* McGraw-Hill, New York, 1970, p. 343. We used Kendall's Tau to determine association and, if any, the direction of the association. For further information see Maurice G. Kendall, *Rank Order Correlation Methods,* Charles Griffin, London, 1970.

24 Each category of practitioners is treated exclusively; the combination category is a 'mixed bag' of M.Ds., marginal, and illegal healers.

25 The findings from Table 2 must be viewed with caution because of the small number of respondents in the young and middle age groups.

26 The culture-of-poverty concept was used here as a heuristic device, i.e. education is not the only measure of the culture of poverty. This term has

been misused in the literature. See Berkanovic and Reeder, 'Ethnic, economic and social psychological factors in the source of medical care', op. cit.
27 The qualitative findings will be further analysed in a forthcoming paper.

Additional Bibliography on Marginal Medicine

Abse, Dannie, *Medicine on Trial,* London: Aldus Books, 1967. See especially Chapter 5, pp. 156-187.

Bernard, Viola W., 'Why people become victims of quackery', *Proceedings of the Second National Congress on Medical Quackery,* Chicago: American Medical Association, 1963.

Bessemans, A., *et al.,* 'Scientific inquest on so-called medical radiaesthesia', *Bruxelles-Medical,* Vol. 28, February 1948.

Cobb, Beatrix, 'Why do people detour to quacks?', in E. Gartly Jaco (ed.), *Patients, Physicians and Illness,* New York: The Free Press, 1958, pp. 283-297.

Coe, Rodney, M., 'Other practitioners of the healing arts', in his *Sociology of Medicine,* New York: McGraw-Hill, 1970.

Fishbein, Morris, *The Medical Follies,* New York: Boni and Liveright, 1925.

Flexner, Abraham, 'A layman's view of osteopathy', *Journal of the American Medical Association,* Vol. 42, June 1914, pp. 1831-1833.

Gardner, Martin, *Fads and Fallacies in the Name of Science,* New York: Dover Books, 1957.

Hoffman, Lois, 'Problem patient; the Christian Scientist', in E. Gartly Jaco (ed.), *Patients, Physicians and Illness,* New York: The Free Press, 1958, pp. 278-283.

Holbrook, Stewart H., *The Golden Age of Quackery,* New York: Macmillan, 1959.

Inglis, Brian, *Fringe Medicine,* London: Faber & Faber, 1964.

Jacobs, Hayes B., 'Oral Roberts: High priest of faith healing', *Harpers Magazine,* No. 224, February 1962, pp. 37-43.

Jameson, Eric, *The Natural History of Quackery,* London: Michael Joseph, 1961.

Jones, Louis C., 'Practitioners of folk medicine', *Bulletin of the History of Medicine,* 23, September-October 1949, pp. 480-493.

Jones, Owen Michael, *Why Faith Healing?,* Ottawa: Mercury Series, Canadian Centre for Folk Culture Studies, National Museum of Canada, 1972.

Kaufman, Martin, *Homeopathy in America: The Rise and Fall of a Medical Heresy,* Baltimore: Johns Hopkins Press, 1971.

Knowles, F. N., 'Some investigations into psychic healing', *Journal of the Institute of the American Society of Psychical Research,* Vol. 48, No. 1, January 1954.

Lauer, Roger M., 'Urban shamans: the influence of folk healers on medical care in our cities', *The New Physician,* August 1973, pp. 486-489.

——, 'A medium for mental health', in Irving I. Zaretsky and Mark P. Leone (eds.), *Religious Movements in Contemporary America,* Princeton: Princeton University Press, 1974, pp. 338-354.

Lerrick, G. P., 'Report on quackery from the FDA', *Proceedings of the National Congress on Medical Quackery,* Chicago: American Medical Association, 1961.

Macklin, June, 'Belief, ritual and healing: New England spiritualism and Mexican-American spiritism compared', in Irving I. Zaretsky and Mark P. Leone (eds.), *Religious Movements in Contemporary America,* Princeton: Princeton University Press, 1974, pp. 383-417.

Moody, Edward J., 'Magical Therapy: an anthropological investigation of contemporary satanism', in Irving I. Zaretsky and Mark P. Leone (eds.), *Religious Movements in Contemporary America,* Princeton: Princeton University Press, 1974, pp. 355-382.

Pattison, Mansell E., *et al.,* 'Faith Healing', *Journal of Nervous and Mental Disease,* Vol. 157, No. 6, 1973, pp. 397-405.

Pattison, Mansell E., 'Ideological support for the marginal middle class: faith healing and glossolalia', in Irving I. Zaretsky and Mark P. Leone (eds.), *Religious Movements in Contemporary America,* Princeton: Princeton University Press, 1974, pp. 418-455.

Paulsen, Alice E., 'Religious healing', *Journal of the American Medical Association,* Vol. 86, May 1926, No. 15, pp. 1519-1524; No. 22, pp. 1617-1623; No. 29, pp. 1692-1697.

Reed, Louis, *The Healing Cults,* Chicago: The University of Chicago Press, 1932.

Rogler, Lloyd H. and Hollingshead, August B., 'The Puerto Rican spiritualist as a psychiatrist', *American Journal of Sociology,* Vol. 67, 1961, pp. 17-21.

Rose, Louis, 'Some aspects of paranormal healing', *British Medical Journal,* December 1954.

——, *Faith Healing,* Harmondsworth: Penguin Books, 1971.

Stekert, Ellen J., 'Focus for conflict: Southern mountain medical beliefs in Detroit', in Americo Paredes and Ellen J. Stekert (eds.), *The Urban Experience and Folk Tradition,* Austin: University of Texas Press, 1971.

Wardwell, Walter I., 'Public regulation of chiropractic', *Journal of the National Medical Association,* Vol. 53, No. 2, March 1961, pp. 166-172.

——, 'Orthodoxy and heterodoxy in medical practice', *Social Science and Medicine,* Vol. 6, 1972, pp. 759-763.

Young, James Harvey, 'Device quackery in America', *Bulletin of the History of Medicine,* Vol. 39, March-April 1965, pp. 154-162.

——, *The Medical Messiahs,* Princeton: Princeton University Press, 1967.

Notes on Contributors

GILLIAN ALLEN, M.A. was formerly a graduate student at the University of Aberdeen. She has conducted research on Pentecostalists, and now lives in Jamaica.

JOHN ALAN LEE, D.Phil. is Associate Professor of Sociology at Scarborough College, University of Toronto. He has published articles on faith healing, styles of loving, and the social effects of television in the classroom. His books include *Sectarian Healers and Hypnotherapy*, Queens Printer, Toronto, 1970; *Test Patterns*, University of Toronto Press, Toronto, 1971; and *Colours of Love*, New Press, Toronto, 1973.

PETER MORLEY, Ph.D. is an Assistant Professor of Medical Sociology in the Department of Community Medicine, Memorial University, Newfoundland. He has engaged in research on Canadian Indians, and overseas Asian communities, and has authored several reports on alcoholism. His current research interests are in the areas of medical belief systems, social psychiatry and health action programmes.

ARTHUR E. NUDELMAN, Ph.D. is Associate Professor of Sociology at Old Dominion University, Virginia. He has published numerous papers on Christian Scientists, health and illness behaviour, and measuring religiosity.

ROBERT QUAN, M.A. is a graduate research assistant at Mississippi State University. He is engaged upon research into Chinese folk healing, sorcerers and sorcery, and deviant health-care practices.

JULIAN B. ROEBUCK, Ph.D. is Professor of Sociology at Mississippi State University. He has written several books, including *Criminal Typology*, Charles C Thomas, Springfield, Illinois, 1967; with Raymond G. Kessler, *The Etiology of Alcoholism*, Charles C Thomas, Springfield, Illinois, 1973; with James B. Cowie, *An Ethnography of a Chiropractic Clinic*, The Free Press, New York, 1975; and with Wolfgang Frese, *The Rendezvous: A Case Study of an After-Hours Club*, The Free Press, New York, 1976.

ROY WALLIS, D.Phil. is Lecturer in Sociology at Stirling University. He has published several articles on religious sects and social

166 *Marginal Medicine*

movements. His book *The Road to Total Freedom: A Sociological Analysis of Scientology* is published by Heinemann Educational Books, London, 1976. He is editor of *Sectarianism: Analyses of Religious and Non-Religious Sects,* Peter Owen, London, and Halsted Press, New York, 1975.

WALTER I. WARDWELL, Ph.D. is Professor of Sociology in the Graduate School, University of Connecticut. He has published widely on chiropractors, Christian Science healing, and the antecedents of heart disease.

Index

Index